Kære Mads,

Tillykke med din nye lejlighed!
Tak fordi du altid er så gæstfri
og fordi vi måtte bo hos dig
denne gang.
Vi nyder altid at slå et smut
forbi vores andet hjem: London!

Abi + Birgit ☺

MIRÓ

MIRÓ

Stephen Butler

STUDIO EDITIONS

To Clare Butler and Andrew John,
with love and gratitude

This edition first published in Great Britain by Studio Editions Ltd.
Princess House, 50 Eastcastle Street
London W1N 7AP

© 1995 Studio Editions Ltd.

Based on *Miró/Les chefs d'œuvre* by Georges Raillard
published by Editions Hazan, Paris, 1989

The right of Stephen Butler to be identified as the author of this work
has been asserted by him in accordance with the Copyright, Designs
and Patents Act, 1988.

The works of Joan Miró are © ADAGP, Paris and
DACS, London 1995

ISBN 1 85170 907 X

Designed by Simon Bell

Printed and bound in Singapore

Frontispiece:
Miró working on a poster for the exhibition *Agora* 1, 1971.
Museum of Modern Art, Strasbourg

INTRODUCTION

The art of Joan Miró is instantly recognizable today to millions of people, as recognizable as that of Vincent Van Gogh, Pablo Picasso or Miró's fellow-Catalan Salvador Dalí. Yet far fewer, perhaps, know anything about him or his life, or know even what he looked like. By no means everybody who admires his work would claim to understand it – not that this is necessarily important. Few would claim to 'understand' the work of Picasso, or of Dalí, any more than they would that of Hieronymus Bosch, or Edvard Munch. Yet the work of all these artists is admired, to some extent *because* it seems mysterious and suggestive rather than straightforward. 'I don't know why, but I like it' is a common reaction to modern painting, in particular to abstract and to Surrealist painting – almost as if we need to apologize for liking it. Modern art is still, for many, dangerous territory; the haunt of intellectual pseudery, élitist criticism, and a disturbing lack of 'common sense' (and nowhere is this more true than of Surrealism, the movement with which Miró was associated for much of his working life). In Miró's case, however, it is perhaps not so difficult to say why people like his paintings. In the first place, they are very colourful. Miró often used bright, primary colours which have a cheerful effect. The shapes he created suggest forms – birds, stars, women – in a simple, direct way which often seems playful and humorous. There is an apparent whimsicality about many of them (a whimsicality often accentuated by the titles of his pictures, such as *The Beautiful Bird Deciphering the Unknown to a Pair of Lovers*). While Miró's work may remain obscure in the sense that the viewer may not be able to understand exactly what he or she is looking at, the works most commonly reproduced are rarely threatening. It is difficult to imagine a Miró provoking the kind of reaction which greeted Carl Andre's *Equivalent VIII* (the so-called 'pile of bricks' in the Tate Gallery), or the sight of a cow cut lengthways with a chainsaw, or the bafflement some people experience when confronted with the work of Jackson Pollock or Mark Rothko. Miró is popular because his art does not seem to demand of us anything other than simple enjoyment.

Yet there is much more to Miró's work than playfulness and wit – though these things are there – and what may seem to us humorous and bright may on closer analysis often turn out to have been born out of anger, doubt and despair. The symbols which are scattered over his canvases may look to some like mere doodling, or an obscure game, but they were part of a concerted intellectual effort, a lifelong struggle to understand the human condition and to communicate his sense of humanity through ceaseless questioning of the nature of language and of representation. The woman and bird which appear in so many of his paintings were not just personal symbols but an attempt to express what he felt to be fundamental truths about the world.

Like many of his fellow-Surrealists, these endeavours involved both a 'scientific' or intellectual impulse and a 'poetic', irrational, even mystical one. In the pursuit of the real, or the surreal, or the absolute, all channels were viable to the Surrealists (though they bickered endlessly about their personal preferences) from Marxism and Freudianism to Fascism and Catholicism. Miró, however, never aligned himself with this tendency or that. He remained stubbornly his own man and although he took from such ideas as much as he needed, he never 'signed up' to any of them. He was a solitary, quiet figure in the feverish world of the Surrealist movement. Whereas many would talk and argue endlessly about their own work – and that of others – getting Miró to discuss his art was like extracting teeth. He was not an intellectual in the sometimes derogatory sense that we use that word today. But he was a man of acute intelligence, a driven, obsessive man, a man of violent emotion yet taciturn and shy.

Before anything else, two things need to be understood about Joan Miró: he was a painter not just by inclination, or because a particular ability suggested a career, but by nature – he expressed himself fully and wholly through his work. And, first, last and always, he was a Catalan.

Miró's roots lay in the countryside of Cataluña, in particular in Tarragona, a region to the south of Barcelona, and in the peasant culture and traditions of that area. The influence of his background upon his work is profound – far more so than is the case with most twentieth-century artists. Miró remained devoted to this inheritance, and made frequent journeys to reimmerse himself in it, to reconnect with the essence of his Catalan identity – Catalan art, Catalan poetry, Catalan soil. A frequently cited example of its importance is that when leaving for Paris as a young man Miró took with him a handful of grass from his parents' farm so that he would not lose touch with its essence while painting his paean to Catalan identity *The Farm* (page 59).[1] 'Everything is measured against Montroig.'[2]

Miró was not born into an agricultural family or community, but peasant life was not far removed in his family history. His father, Miguel Miró y Adzerias, a Barcelona watchmaker and jeweller, was the son of a village blacksmith and a migrant to Barcelona from the village of Cornudella in Tarragona. His mother, Dolores Ferra i Oromi, was the daughter of a cabinet-maker in

Palma, Mallorca. Most of the wider family of aunts, uncles and cousins were still rural people, and from the earliest age Joan was familiar with both the Tarragonese countryside and the Mediterranean island. These places and their people were to remain important to him, even sustain him spiritually, all his life.

He was born on 20th April 1893, at a time when Barcelona was approaching the height of its redevelopment from a once powerful medieval port into a bustling cosmopolitan centre. As the capital of Cataluña, Barcelona has always proudly exhibited its difference from the rest of Spain, and in particular from the centre of power, Madrid and its Castilian culture. Like many places which form the focus of a 'nation within a nation', Barcelona determinedly resisted the status of a 'regional capital' within Spain and the subsidiarity which that implies; the city's art, architecture and culture fused Catalan and international elements to foster and amplify the Cataluñan sense of identity, often in defiance of Spanish law. Catalan poetry and literature had been banned for long periods of its history, as indeed was the spoken language itself from time to time[3] – a state of affairs which recurred under the Fascist dictatorship of Franco during this century. The cultural climate of Cataluña at the time of Miró's birth resembled that of Ireland before the Easter Rising. A similar cultural censorship had been enforced, and a comparable circle of urban artists and intellectuals saw themselves as the guardians of an ancient and oppressed national identity rooted in a peasant culture and threatened by a distant political centre.

Internationalism in Barcelona manifested itself most strikingly in the success of three architects, Lluis Domenech i Montaner, Josep Puig i Cadafalch and, most importantly, Antoni Gaudí i Cornet, all practitioners of what was known as *modernisme* – the Catalan variant of the movement known as art nouveau. Their success was the result, above all, of the simultaneous happy emergence of a renewed Catalan patriotism and a large and wealthy bourgeoisie in the second half of the nineteenth century. The bourgeoisie

The Pedicure *1901*
Pencil, watercolour and ink on paper. 11.6 x 11.7 cm
Fundacio Miró, Barcelona

---

needed to express their Cataluñan difference from the rest of Spain, but they also needed to define themselves as an urban class, higher and more cultured than their peasant forebears. Ideologically disinclined to look toward the Castilian ethos of Madrid for inspiration, they turned outward, with the result that Barcelona became one of the most modern and cosmopolitan cities in Europe.

Miró rarely spoke of his childhood in any detail, and we know far less about it than we do of Picasso's early days, for example. No doubt this is in part due to the fact that his parents did not wish him to become an artist – unlike Picasso's, who were proud of their son's abilities. Miró said: 'There was a total separation between me and my parents. I felt this in a very painful, violent way. But I'm also very happy about it because those difficulties gave me muscles'.[4] It seems that it was toward his father that Joan had the strongest antipathy: 'My mother had a strong personality and was very intelligent. I was always very close to her, [but] my father...was absolutely the opposite'.[5] His father seems to have been an earnest, buttoned-up, stolid man, who made fun of his son's vivid imagination. Joan's health may have been delicate[6] though it was robust in adulthood. He had a younger sister, Dolores, to whom he was close.

He showed an enthusiasm for drawing (though no exceptional skill) from about 1901. His earliest surviving pictures, now in the Fundacio Miró in Barcelona, are careful, colourful drawings of animals, flowers, and street scenes, many produced on his family holidays in Cornudella and Palma. There is also a cartoon-like drawing of the interior of a chiropodist's shop, with the chiropodist working on a patient's foot which, in the absence of very much other evidence, some critics have seized upon as early evidence of an obsession with feet. Feet and shoes feature in many of his later works, where they sometimes have a symbolic role (*Still Life with Old Shoe*, 1937) and are often grotesquely distorted (*The Farmer's Wife*, 1922). In Freudian theory shoes are usually held to be symbolic of the vagina, and the foot therefore has a phallic role. While Miró was quite obviously obsessed with female genitalia, feet and footwear are more often symbolic of contact with the earth in his paintings. Around the time that he started school he also took private drawing lessons. Surviving sketchbooks display a workmanlike but unexceptional ability. There are no figure drawings, a subject he always found difficult. These lessons were certainly his mother's idea. In school he was an unexceptional pupil, dreamy and bored.

The family seem to have been comfortably off; there is no indication of any hardship. However, when later in life Miró heard his father described as 'a goldsmith' he scoffed and called him 'a repairer of watches'. This may have been less than charitable; in 1910 they bought a farmhouse at Montroig (pronounced 'Montrotch') in the countryside south of Barcelona, for use as a holiday-home, which implies a relatively high income. This can be seen as an attempt to re-establish the family's sense of their country heritage by purchasing a traditional home, a *casa pairal*, to anchor their unfamiliar status in the new urban middle-class. Despite their closeness to the land they were very definitely a bourgeois family; when Miró himself had become a famous artist he was frequently described as 'a bourgeois' by those meeting him for the first time and expecting some wild, Surrealist bohemian. His dress remained conservative, his studio scrupulously tidy, his manner dignified and reserved all his life. Above all, his commitment to work was almost certainly inherited from his father. Many artists refer to their 'work' but are only intermittently productive. Miró always worked hard, both physically and mentally.

When Joan was fourteen the family was faced with a choice; it was time for him to go to secondary school, and the type of school chosen even at that age set the scholar firmly on the way to a particular career. Miguel insisted that Joan go to the Commercial School and prepare himself for a life in business. He had no confidence in his son's ability to support himself as an artist. Besides, both his *nouveau bourgeois* status and his peasant ancestry would have told him that artists were neither hard-working nor 'respectable', that they were womanizing drunkards and layabouts with dangerously radical political ideas. Joan never forgave his father's lack of faith.

The family reached a compromise, however, and in addition to his business studies Miró enrolled at the Barcelona School of Art, known as the *Llotja* (lodge) because it was housed on the top floor of the building of that name which was chiefly occupied by the Stock Exchange. The Llotja was for its time an enlightened and liberal place. Miró's principal teachers were Modest Urgell Inglada, a follower of the 'Olot School' of Spanish artists who admired the French Barbizon painters, and Josep Pasco Marisa, who taught the decorative arts. As mentioned earlier, in Barcelona that meant a prolonged exposure to the principles of art nouveau, and Miró's two surviving designs (for brooches) are in that style. One of the reasons Miró's father tolerated the lessons seems to have been that he thought the applied art studies would be useful to his jewellery business.

Miró formed good relationships with both teachers. They were open-minded, and pupils were encouraged to be original, to discuss the latest developments, and, within certain boundaries, to find their own way. This indicates a distinct liberalization of the regime since the days when Picasso had been a pupil, and Picasso's father

had been a teacher, over a decade earlier[7]. Then the atmosphere was described as 'stultifying'. However, the drawing lessons, in which pupils had to concentrate on studying plaster-casts of antique sculpture, remained old-fashioned and very dry. How Miró performed in them is not known. Perhaps, as a part-timer, he was not forced to take them. The drawings that survive are mostly copies of the work of Urgell. Some critics have suggested that Urgell's open, somewhat featureless landscapes taught Miró a great deal about the positioning of objects on a canvas, and that the sense of space in his later work is a legacy of this time[8]. Although there are many Mirós in which the canvas is packed with detail, in addition to the many uncluttered ones, the point may be valid.

Pasco undoubtedly encouraged his pupils to study contemporary developments in Barcelona, and Miró spent many hours studying the art-nouveau architecture

---

Parque Guell
Barcelona
Antoni Gaudí

of the city. In particular the park bequeathed to the city by the industrialist Guell, with pavilions and benches by his protégé Antoni Gaudí, fascinated the young artist. The sinuous lines and fantastic metamorphic structures of Gaudí's buildings influenced a generation of Spanish artists – notably Salvador Dalí, who in the 1920s wrote a tribute to Gaudí as a precursor of Surrealism. To Miró and his friends, however, Gaudí provided an inspiration not just in a formal sense, but because it was plain to them that it was possible to pursue such a deeply personal vision and succeed. Gaudí was far from universally popular in Barcelona, and was almost unknown outside Spain for decades afterward, but his buildings, thanks to the influence of Guell, were testimony to the possibilities of the modern movement, uniting functionality with an uncompromising aesthetic.

Pasco's most significant gift to his pupil, however, was undoubtedly the interest he fostered in Catalan folk art. This rich and varied field continued to provide inspiration for Miró for the next seven decades. Since they emanated from a peasant society, these traditional arts were not just to be seen in museums, but were still part of everyday life outside the cities, and intimately bound up with Cataluñan ideas of identity and history.

Miró became a devotee of several aspects of Catalan folk art, besides that of Mallorca. Historically, Cataluña had had close political and racial ties with the Pyrenean regions of Spain and, beyond those, with southern France. With a great port as its capital, it had always been open to the wider world of the Mediterranean as well. So, within the chequered history of Spain as a whole, with its successive layers of Celtic, Roman, Gothic, Norman and Arab influence, the Catalan region had its own unique cultural variations[9]. Most important to Miró were the remarkable frescoes to be found in churches across the region. Mixing Romanesque and local elements, these form a powerful canon of images which were designed not just to illustrate the stories of the Bible to an illiterate peasantry, as medieval church paintings did right across Europe, but to communicate the awesome power of God in no uncertain terms. They

have the directness of propaganda, intended to cow the viewer into religious observance. Their effect on Miró – who visited the collection in the Catalan Museum of Folk Art every year of his life, except in the darkest years of the Franco regime – was profound. Both formally, in their treatment of line and volume, and as an expression of the indigenous Catalan spirit, these anonymous paintings form a vital element in the formation of Miró's mature aesthetic. Robert Hughes, in his history of Barcelona, illustrates this connexion: 'Miró always loved the metaphoric, the bestial, the fabulous. And…the hard wiry outlines of Catalan Romanesque painting, the flat declarative shapes silhouetted on clear background fields of colour, the way that widely separated forms energise the flatness between them – all this seems deeply Miróesque. But of course it is better to say that Miró was deeply Romanesque.'

Hughes also suggests that the eyes, which are a recurring feature in Miró's work, have their origin in Catalan tradition, and in the concept of the *mirada fuerte*, or 'strong look', in Spanish peasant culture. The eyes and the gaze were powerfully magical. The 'strong look' is the unblinking gaze which sees into the mind, or the soul; the gaze which can 'put the evil eye' on its recipient. It is an essential component of machismo – Picasso knew that his dark, penetrating eyes had the *mirada fuerte*, as many photographs testify. In Cataluñan frescoes, Christ is shown gazing down on the congregation with this unflinching, all-seeing gaze. Miró's own work is full of eyes, not just as parts of human figures but also attached to trees and inanimate objects, and the concept of looking at the world around him, of seeing with an almost supernatural intensity, is central to his art. (The name 'Miró', coincidentally, means 'the looker'.) As he remarked to the art historian Walter Erben, 'Everything comes from the visible. The object claims my attention more and more. There is nothing abstract in my pictures.'[10]

After three years at the Commercial School Miró went to work as an apprentice book-keeper in a hardware firm, Dalmau y Oliveras. He was miserable there: so miserable that after only a few months he became acutely depressed, and fell ill. The accounts of this period vary. Some writers relate that he had 'a fever'; one that it was a 'typhoid-like' fever; and one that he actually had 'typhoid fever'[11]. Another states boldly that he suffered a 'complete nervous breakdown'[12], which he plainly did not. It seems likely that his acute depression triggered psychosomatic symptoms (which is not to say that the physical illness was not serious – evidently it was) or laid him open to the kind of infection common in such cases of stress and at a similar age, such as glandular fever. In any event the combination of mental and physical illness was enough to rescue him permanently from the world of wage slavery; he was sent to convalesce at his parents' farmhouse at Montroig and there he made a rapid and complete recovery. There too he made up his mind to be a painter and nothing else. His father, convinced by these events that Joan would never be a businessman, conceded defeat. This version of events, however, conveniently ignores Miró's own testimony, that he was 'fired' from the hardware company 'for drawing in the ledgers' and succeded in his desire to become an artist only after a struggle with the family[13]. Whether or not this preceded the illness is unclear.

After his convalescence Miró enrolled in a private art school run by Francesc Gali. The atmosphere there was freer than at the Llotja, and there was a considerable amount of al fresco teaching out in the city and the surrounding countryside. There were debates, musical evenings and poetry readings; the school was a meeting-point for Barcelona's aspiring avant-garde. Among Miró's new acquaintances were three who remained lifelong friends: Josep Llorens Artigas, Enric Ricart Nin and Josep Rafols Fontanals. Of these, Artigas seems to have been the dominant personality. Miró, with his quiet and thoughtful disposition, was never cut out to be a leader or the focus of a group. In later years, when Miró was an internationally famous artist, he and Artigas – by then an established ceramicist and potter – were to collaborate on many projects.

Gali was, for the time, a surprisingly liberal and experimental teacher. He would never have found employment in a conventional art school. Miró remembered how on walks in the countryside Gali would actually forbid his students to draw, telling them to *look* instead (a very Catalan attitude). In an episode which Miró frequently recounted, Gali instinctively diagnosed Miró's difficulty in reproducing three-dimensional form; he blindfolded his student, gave him an object to handle, then removed the object and put it away. The blindfold was removed and Miró had to draw the object. Not many teachers of drawing at that time would have been able to think in such a lateral way, and the episode was one which Miró evidently felt shaped his thinking significantly, and laid the foundation for a distinguished career in sculpture. Again and again Miró refers to his work as a process of drawing on and transforming a kind of natural energy, the energy of the earth, as if he were engaged in shaping a natural force. Such a telluric source could not be seen, of course; it had to be felt, to be absorbed from his surroundings. There is a connection here between eyesight and other forms of 'seeing' – touching, imagining, feeling, dreaming. Miró's art – abstracted, not abstract – reproduces the results of this attempt to 'see' completely, to encompass his subjects.

Gali had faith in Miró's ability; as he later told Jacques Dupin, he would inform Miró's doubting father every week, 'Your son will be successful, he will be a great artist.'[14] Some indication of the volte-face in his family's attitudes, and perhaps of the strength of Miró's ambition, is that after leaving the hardware company Miró never seems to have taken any other employment, and must have been supported by his parents, however reluctantly. His sister bought him paints when he was short of money. He continued to study at Gali's until 1915, and also enrolled in another school, the Cercle Artistic de Sant Lluc, until 1918, by which time he was 25 years old.

Barcelona was firmly established as Spain's most progressive city, and Miró would have been familiar with many of the artistic developments occurring in

Virgin with Child
Detail of a mural in the nave of the
Church of San Pedro de Sorpe, c. 1125
The Museum of Art, Cataluna

Paris in the post-Cubist era. After all, two of the key figures in the Parisian avant-garde were Spaniards – Picasso and Juan Gris – and this must have predisposed the young Barcelonese to an enthusiasm for Cubism. Picasso occasionally returned to Barcelona, but Miró never had the audacity even to approach him there, though his mother knew Picasso's mother very well[15]. The major modern gallery in the city, Dalmau's, held exhibitions of work by the Parisian avant-garde; in 1912, for example, Miró would have seen work by Laurencin, Léger and Gris. Yet there can be no doubt that a certain chauvinism would have also influenced Miró and his friends, in that Barcelonese modernism – the modernism of art nouveau – must have seemed to them the point from which, as Catalans, they should go forward. It is known that Miró was an admirer particularly of Gaudí, and it is difficult to imagine at this stage that he would have contemplated turning his back on this tradition. At least one source claims, intriguingly, that Gaudí (who died in 1926) was himself, as an old man, a student in the drawing class at the Cercle Artistic alongside Miró[16].

Miró's sketchbooks from this period show a fascination with the circus and the music-hall, perhaps evidence of an enthusiasm for the work of the Impressionists or even Picasso's 'Blue' and 'Rose' period work of *c.* 1900-1905. There are many figure-studies and life-drawings, testimony to his awareness that these were the weakest aspect of his work. In contrast to the sometimes quite polished copies of Urgell's work he had produced while at the Llotja seven or eight years previously, many of his sketches from 1914 and 1915 appear stiff and even clumsy. He may have been looking at the work of another artist for whom figures presented difficulties, Paul Cézanne; Miró uses similar long ovoid forms to delineate limbs and body masses.

Despite Barcelona's cosmopolitanism it was inevitable that it should remain something of a backwater in international terms, and it is not surprising that we find, in Miró's first mature catalogued painting, *The Peasant* (1914), a vivacious but unpromising impressionism of the kind that had been abandoned by young Parisian artists a decade earlier. It is a weak picture, though it has energy and vibrant colour; a bravura performance by a young man who does not have the technique to bring it off. Similar awkwardness can be seen in the two figure studies reproduced (pages 29 & 53), in which the confidence of the execution cannot save the results from mediocrity. But Miró seems to have realized early on that his strengths lay elsewhere, and that he should play on them. A landscape of 1916, a view of part of Barcelona's old quarter and city wall called *The Reform*, is a competent performance, in which blocks of shadowed and sunlit architectural mass are enlivened by his startling use of azure for the deepest shadows. Cézanne is the clearest influence on the picture's organization, but by now Miró had also encountered Fauvist painting, and learned from Matisse that the bold colouring for which he had always had an instinctive talent could be put to effective use.

The advent of the First World War in the autumn of 1914 brought to an abrupt end the developing avant-garde scene in Paris. The market for modern art dried up as the rich fled the war and rapid inflation and put their money in safe Swiss bank accounts. Many of the leading young artists in Paris had been foreigners – Spaniards, Russians and Italians – who now found themselves unwelcome in a France steeped in patriotic fervour. The Germans were suddenly 'enemy aliens', and many went to Switzerland or to America rather than face repatriation or internment. Thus for the duration of the war the focus of the avant-garde was fragmented in various countries where progressive artists formed nucleii of radicalism; in Berlin, New York, Brussels, Paris and in Zurich, where a group of chiefly ex-Parisian residents instigated the movement which was to become known as 'Dada'.

Dada crystallized around a Zurich club, the Cabaret Voltaire, and events there organized by the Swiss artist Richard Hulsenbeck, the German writer Hugo Ball and the Romanian poet Tristan Tzara. It was an anti-movement rather than a movement: anti-art, anti-sense, anti-politics. It has been described as 'nihilistic', but this implies that its chief urge was destructive. That was true only in the sense that the artists and writers involved wanted to 'destroy' their inheritance of academicism and the bourgeoisie's deadening influence on the art market. It was a movement of incredible productivity, with scores of small pamphlets and journals, reams of chiefly humorous and nonsensical poetry and prose and, despite the privations of wartime, a continuous outpouring of experimental painting and sculpture. Dada threw away the rule-book, but only to enable artists to write their own. It was at root an attempt to provide an alternative to a cultural tradition which the participants felt had been hand-in-hand with the political system which had led them into the disaster of the war. Very quickly a kind of international underground grew up, and the Zurich-based group discovered like-minded artists in other cities: Max Ernst in Cologne, Kurt Schwitters in Hamburg, Marcel Duchamp in New York. Magazines kept these artists in contact with each other; very active on this front was the extraordinary figure of Francis Picabia.

Born in 1879, Picabia came from a wealthy background and had been active as a painter since the early years of the century, without too much success. He is thought to have painted the first pure abstract picture, in 1907 or 1908, thus predating Kandinsky's original pure form-and-colour experiments by a year. Originally an Impressionist (as indeed had been his Dadaist colleague Duchamp), he joined the Cubist group known as the *Section d'Or* (Golden Section) in 1912, again with Duchamp. This group held to a form of Cubism in which the geometrical disposition of elements within a picture were believed to provide a key to the expression of absolute rules of aesthetic beauty, giving painting a status akin to that of music. (The Golden Section after which the group named itself was a mystical mathematical measure known since the Renaissance.) Picabia, however, was not someone for whom such an essentially serious enterprise could have lasting appeal. He had a sideline in producing mildly pornographic nudes for the Algiers art market, and liked to project an image of an international playboy. His wealth gave him considerable freedom during the war, and his age kept him from conscription. It was Picabia who formed the link between the isolated groups of artists. He was included in the notorious Armory Show in New York in 1914 which introduced Dada to an aghast America, and founded the Dada journal *291,* named after the gallery of the avant-garde photographer Alfred Stieglitz. Back in Europe he went to Paris and Zurich before arriving in 1917 in Barcelona, to live there for a few months and to produce another journal, *391.*

Miró meanwhile had rented his first studio, with his friend Enric Ricart, and continued his Sant Lluc studies, exhibiting three paintings at the group's 1915 exhibition. In 1915 he was faced with military conscription. Although his father could have paid to have Joan exempted, he chose not to, and Miró served three months in the army from October to December, an interruption repeated in each of the next three years.

In 1916 the Parisian art dealer Ambroise Vollard brought a large exhibition of recent French art to Dalmau's gallery in Barcelona. Here Miró saw works by Picasso, Matisse, Gris, Braque and others, including Gleizes and Metzinger[17], then considered the two leading theorists of Cubism, or 'simultaneism'. Picabia's arrival meant, however, that Miró came into contact for the first time with somebody at the forefront of the avant-garde. The young Catalan artists would meet at Dalmau's gallery to have long conversations with Picabia and with other exiles from the war, and to read the avant-garde journals and magazines – *Nord-Sud* (founded by the poet Pierre Reverdy, later a Surrealist, with André Breton, the founder of Surrealism, and Tristan Tzara, the prime mover of Dadaist literature), *Les Soirées de Paris,* and *L'Instant,* as well as *391.* Miró, however, did not commit himself artistically to the new anti-establishment, and remained set on his course of methodically assimilating the lessons of recent French art. Apart from Matisse and the Fauves, Cézanne and Van Gogh are the chief influences on his work at this time, which was developing restlessly but with increasing confidence. In

The Beach at Montroig (1916, page 45), a calm scene in a muted palette, several influences – Impressionism, Pointillism and the 'empty' Böcklinian landscapes of his teacher Urgell – seem to be present. A year later, *Nord-Sud* (page 47) is a vibrant pastiche of Matisse, though marked by a certain lack of overall cohesion. The presence of the avant-garde journal to which the title of the painting refers, visible on the table alongside the works of Goethe, demonstrates vividly that Miró, while involved in the circle around Dalmau and Picabia and familiar with radical art, was more cautious in his own approach; it is a kind of joke, since the Dadaist journal is a Cubist device in a Fauvist picture.

In the same year, *The Church at Ciurana* (1917, page 49) is an assured, well-organized painting, bringing together the influences of Cézanne, Van Gogh and Matisse in a convincing and attractive unified style, but ten years or more behind the Parisian lead. Other landscapes of that year, painted in his beloved Montroig and in other villages in the environs of Barcelona, carry forward these influences into a more angular, still more brightly coloured style, highly patterned with facets and strips of flat paint, less expressionistic but still quite traditional in terms of perspective. In a letter to his friend Ricart he speaks of his 'solitary life' in the countryside, and of 'the marvellously primitive nature of the people, the intense work, spiritual contemplation and the possibility in a world created by my isolated spirit, like Dante, far from all material realities'.[18] This is a firmly nineteenth-century view of the artist, far removed from the metropolitanism of Cubism and the urban anarchy of Dada. The reference to Dante is telling; Miró was a fervent reader of poetry all his life.

If Picabia's presence did not radicalize Miró's art, it did nevertheless introduce him to radical thinking, and must have convinced him, if he was not already decided, that his future lay outside Barcelona. And while Dadaism had no contemporary effect, it is typical of Miró that he should have observed and stored up its lessons, which, as he himself related, were to have an influence on his work some years later, in the 1920s.[19]

During 1917 and 1918 he produced a series of portraits, nine in all, stubbornly working away at what he still perceived to be his weakest point, the figure. Once again Cézanne and Van Gogh are the chief formal influences, but the colour is determinedly fauvist. Beginning with a loose, expressionist-influenced brushwork, as had the landscapes, the series is marked by a progression toward a more ordered, patterned surface. In the portrait of his close friend and studio partner Ricart (page 51) he has arrived at a point where only the face and hands contain any element of loose brushwork, with the picture dominated by the extravagant stripes of the jacket. Miró provides a clue to the thinking behind this progression in the Japanese print placed behind the sitter; he refers to the Japanese work which had deeply influenced late nineteenth and early twentieth century French artists from Toulouse-Lautrec and Degas to Picasso and Matisse, but he also points to the organization of Japanese prints – their non-Western perspective, patterned surface and saturated areas of colour – as an influence on his own painting. This concern with the surface of the picture intensifies in such paintings as *Standing Female Nude* (1918, page 53) where the intense patterning of the carpets, again based on Matisse, disturbs our reading of the position of the female figure, whose body is not a collection of flat areas but of rounded semi-geometrical masses. (The figure is, however, 'cubistic' rather than strictly cubist – the parts of the body are simplified and formalized but the perspective is traditional. Miró may have read Gleizes and Metzinger's *Du Cubisme*, and he had certainly seen their work – see footnote 17.) The perspective is further disrupted by the inclusion of a very stylized, very flat 'cubist' passage on the right.

Contact with Dalmau brought reward in the form of his first one-man show, of 64 works, early in 1918. The exhibition was not a success outside his own small circle of acquaintances. In the same year he joined a coterie headed by his friend Artigas which called themselves the 'Courbet Group'. This is a rather puzzling title, but perhaps referred to Gustave Courbet's strongly anti-academic stance. The group did not last long (although certainly mounted one group show in Barcelona), and we know nothing of its aims or ideology.

Meanwhile Miró's painting was entering a new phase; he spent the summer at Montroig, from whence he wrote to Ricart that what interested him above all 'is the calligraphy of a tree or the tiles on a roof; leaf by leaf, branch by branch, blade by blade of grass'[20]. His colours became more muted, and no longer functioned expressionistically, and he adopted a fine, sinuous line in place of the thick black outlining he had favoured previously. The *Portrait of a Young Girl* (page 57) and a *Self-Portrait*, (page 15), typify this restrained approach in portraiture, but it was in landscape painting that this new style (which he later christened his 'detailist' period) bore the ripest fruit. The first 'detailist' picture was *The Kitchen Garden with Donkey* (1918, page 55), a view of the farmhouse and its garden at Montroig. Here the expressionism and fauvism of his previous landscapes have vanished; no longer is the canvas made up of a series of quasi-geometrical areas of bright colour. Instead, as he intimates in the letter, his concern is the fine delineation of the separate leaves of trees and plants, not in a naturalistic, but in an almost naive manner. His word 'calligraphic' marks the first step toward the experimental paintings of his Surrealist period – he was beginning to explore the relationship between the object and the sign representing that object, and thus between thing and word, word and language. The palette borrows from Cubism in its ochres and browns, but the most surprising innovation is the disruption of the distinction between 'earth' and 'sky'. Areas of ploughed land are placed among the clouds above the farmhouse, suggestive not only of surrounding hills but of a desire to paint not just a view but a summary of the place, the totality of his experience of it. In the meantime he was full of a new confidence and excitement. Miró had entered upon his maturity as a painter.

Self-portrait *1919*
Oil on canvas. 73 x 60 cm
Musée Picasso, Paris

He set out on his first trip to Paris at the end of the war, in March 1919. On arrival, however, he confessed that he was so overwhelmed by the experience that his 'hand froze' and he could do no work, not even at the life-study classes he had planned, with typical level-headedness, to attend. He had brought from Barcelona his *Self-Portrait*, probably with the express intention of showing it to Picasso. On his second day he summoned up the nerve to visit the great man; he had also brought, as an entrée, a cake from Picasso's mother. He was warmly received: 'From the first moment, he was interested in me. He spoke to everyone – the dealers [Daniel-Henri] Kahnweiler and [Paul] Rosenberg – about me; he was very generous that way. But it didn't work.'[21] He gave Picasso, according to some sources, the *Self-Portrait*[22]. Thus began a lifelong mutual respect, which never quite became close friendship. They spoke Catalan together. Miró explored the dealerships and galleries, spent hours in the Louvre (the first major collection he had ever seen – he had never been to Madrid), and returned to Barcelona after a fortnight.

The Courbet Group staged an exhibition at Dalmau's. Like Miró's one-man show, it was unsuccessful. One local artist remarked, 'If this is art, I'm Velasquez.' Miró went to Montroig, where he painted another landscape, *Montroig: The Church and Village*, oddly a return to his Fauvist, pre-detailist style. Perhaps his confidence in himself had been shaken by what he had seen in Paris. In the autumn and winter he worked on a series of still-lives, *The Card Game*, *The Horse, Pipe and Red Flower*, *The Bunch of Grapes* and *The Table*, also known as *Still Life with Rabbit*. As with the *Standing Female Nude* (page 53), these are an uneasy mix of cubist and realist styles. *The Table* (1920) incorporates highly detailed objects – a fish, a cockerel, a rabbit, vine leaves, a red pepper – on an antique farmhouse kitchen table, richly carved, which in turn is placed against a

---

Montroig: The Church and Village *1919*
Oil on canvas. 73 x 61 cm
Dolores Miró de Punyet Collection

geometricized, completely aperspectival background. It also has a strong flavour, significantly, of folk art. The picture works quite successfully despite this clash of elements. The objects stand out vividly against the less interpretable patterning, and the implication is that Miró intends us to concentrate on these objects rather than on an appreciation of the painting as a 'composition'. This is a concern he expressed in his letter to Ricart about the calligraphy of his environment and its minute features, and which he would shortly take to an extreme. At the end of the winter his impatience to get back to Paris got the better of him.

In the spring of 1920 Miró moved permanently to Paris. He sublet a studio at 45 rue Blomet from a fellow-Catalan, the sculptor Pau Gargallo, who taught at the Llotja for most of the year. Miró planned to spend his summers at Montroig, when Gargallo needed his Paris studio. For the first time in his life he was suddenly very poor. He recalled that he only ate a proper lunch once a week. He bought a minimum of essential household objects at the fleamarket, but kept his spartan studio spotlessly clean and tidy, to the amazement of his bohemian friends. Llorens y Artigas was also in the city, and introduced him to the expatriate Catalan community there, but Miró was not 'clubbable' by nature. It was probably Artigas who first took him to one of the Dadaist events Tristan Tzara had begun to organize. Miró was chiefly an onlooker at these soirées. He confessed, however, that he preferred the Dadaist's nonsense to the earnest conservatism of his fellow exiles, who were 'stealing from Renoir' or producing 'watered-down Matisse'[23]. He went so far as to produce a stuffed monkey, mounted on card, and labelled 'Portrait of Cézanne, Rembrandt and Renoir'. But there is no indication that he regarded this as work.

Miró frequently visited Picasso, with whom he had long conversations and who again seemed eager to help his compatriot, but although he had previously regarded the older painter with a certain starry-eyed wonder, he began to change his mind. He disapproved of what he saw as Picasso's blatant commercialism, likening him to a ballerina with many lovers, though he admitted his works were 'very fine' and that he was 'a great painter'.[24] Dismayed by what French artists – even Matisse – were producing, he felt that 'the new Catalan art' was the only trend which held out hope.

When Gargallo returned for the summer Miró retreated to Montroig, presumably to work out this 'new Catalan art'. There he began a view of the house similar in conception to *The Kitchen Garden*, abandoning the fauvist style of his landscape of the previous summer, but retaining a bright palette. At the end of the summer, he returned to the rue Blomet bearing the canvas and an envelope of grass from Montroig, a piece of sympathetic magic to enable him to finish the painting in the same spirit in which it had been begun. Completed early in 1922, *The Farm* (page 59), marks the maturity of his detailist period. His friends were universally dismissive: one even advised him to cut it into pieces and sell them separately.

It is not difficult to understand why. *The Farm* resembled nothing that anyone had seen before. Neither Cubist nor realist, nor Dadaist, the painting presents in a bone-dry style a catalogue of objects, some almost diagrammatic, others painstakingly three-dimensional, all rendered in the harsh sunlight of high summer. It is a completely personal picture which makes no concessions to either traditional or contemporary art. Miró, dismayed at what he saw as the decadence of recent French art, retreated into the certainties of his youth. Unable to identify even with his hero Picasso, he presents the things which make up himself, or at least the true Catalan he wanted to be. Whether or not he believed that this sentimental nationalism could really have such broad appeal as to revivify modern art is open to question. It is more likely that Miró had simply, in the face of the perceived 'bourgeois' dominance of the art market, decided in the best tradition of the romantic artist to go it alone.

The Farm, Robert Hughes writes, is an 'expatriate's painting'. It combines 'the intense...immediate experience of one's homeland and an equally extreme longing for it...[it is] a kind of visual accountancy, an exact toting up and tallying of everything...it could be the pictorial form of the meticulous inventory that went with peasant marriage contracts.' The picture's extreme clarity 'produces the effect of looking down the wrong end of a telescope, so that the scene is remote as well. Hence *The Farm*'s power as an image of nostalgia for what is distant but vivid and dear, for the sights, smells and sounds of childhood. Such longings are known in Catalan as *enyoranca*'[25]. Such indeed has been the traditional reading of the painting, and broadly this is undoubtedly true. However, Hughes probably overstates the personal at the expense of the aesthetic in his analysis. After all, the farm at Montroig was never really Miró's home, nor that of his parents, however fond he was of it. (When he later moved back to Spain he chose to live in the flat in Barcelona, not at Montroig.) Montroig wasn't purchased until Miró was seventeen years old. The objects described so meticulously in the picture are there not as childhood mementoes but as symbols of a Catalan identity which Miró wished to celebrate, which he undoubtedly wished he could truly call his own, but from which he had been removed not only by his residence in Paris but by his family's urban background. Furthermore, he always intended to spend at least part of each year at Montroig – he was not trapped in Paris. So although there is a sense of loss and removal in the picture, we should not forget that it was begun *in situ*. The emotional charge of the picture is indeed that of *enyoranca*, but it is a longing for a past which is as much mythic and nationalistic – and rose-tinted – as personal and specific. The 'new Catalan art' (whatever that meant for him) was probably as great an impetus as his personal feelings.

The importance of *The Farm* in understanding Miró's mature work can hardly be exaggerated, not least because he himself saw it as his first truly successful picture. He worked on it eight hours a day for eight months. 'I suffered terribly, horribly, like a condemned man. I wiped out a lot...getting rid of foreign influences and getting in touch with Cataluña'[26]. At the very centre

Table with Glove *1921*
Oil on canvas. 116.8 x 89.5 cm
The Museum of Modern Art, New York

of the picture's perspective is a figure – tiny, squatting, with arms outstretched – which has puzzled art historians for decades. Most took it to be the baby of the woman slightly behind it. But Hughes has convincingly identified it as a traditional figure from the Catalan peasants' Christmas crib, who in a corner of the stable where the Messiah is born, is quietly relieving himself [27]. This pagan and subversive interloper, the *Caganer* (shitter), is a fertility symbol, linking the Christian story with much older beliefs. As such he is a perfect symbol for Miró at this time, asserting basic principles, Catalan identity, continuity, fecundity, and, metaphorically, defecating on modern art. *The Farm* was shown at the 1922 Salon d'Automne to an indifferent public. It hung in a Montmartre cafe for a

while; it was later bought by Ernest Hemingway, who recognized in it the essence of his own love for Spain.

Clearly Miró had found a rich vein on which to draw. Clearly, too, he would receive little or no encouragement in doing so. *The Farm* drew a line under the detailist period and his painting moved on into further stylistic experiment, but he retained his grip on Cataluña as the subject matter of his work, the emotional engine which motivated him. His next pictures mark a gradual advance from scrupulous realism toward a completely personal depiction of form and space. *The Farmer's Wife* (1922) shows as it were the female figure in *The Farm* in her kitchen, holding a dead rabbit, a basket over the other arm. Whereas her head and body are roughly in proportion, however, Miró has given her elephantine bare feet which, in contrast to her dress, are flatly painted instead of modelled and shaded. These symbolize the strength of her contact with the earth, and thus the simplicity and purity of her (Catalan) spirit. Despite her clothes, her breasts are also clearly defined. She is the first manifestation of the Woman who was to be the subject of hundreds of Miró's works thereafter – or perhaps one should say 'the object'.

Miró's neighbours in the rue Blomet included a circle of writers, poets and painters some of whom were soon to be part of the Surrealist group: Michel Leiris, André Masson, Georges Limbour, Antonin Artaud and Armand Salacrou. As yet they were merely a disparate group, linked by their status as bohemian outsiders, on the fringes of the Dada movement but each with their own interests and concerns. One thing in particular united them: a desire to explore new means of expression. Masson and Miró became close friends, although they were opposites in terms of personality. The Frenchman was a victim of the war, psychologically damaged, who was 'in permanent revolt against society'[28]. He took large quantities of drugs, aiming to disrupt his senses completely in order to achieve a kind of ecstatic frenzy in his work. Oddly enough Miró, the scrupulous and ordered worker, empathized closely with Masson's violence. He refers at times to the violence of his own creativity; when he was having trouble with a painting, he once said, he banged his head against the wall until the blood flowed.

Masson was deeply interested in exploring the subconscious and in the images which flowed from it when he achieved his trance-like states. Inevitably he soon came to the attention of André Breton, a poet whose interest in the world of dreams and the irrational part of the mind stemmed from his studies under the pioneering psychologist Charcot, whose work on hysteria had influenced Freud. With Dada fizzling out as its associated artists pursued their own paths, Breton was attempting to rally the avant-garde into the pursuit of 'the marvellous', to find liberation in art through the deliberate censorship of rationality and an openness to subconscious impulses. Masson was impressed, and it was doubtless he who introduced Miró to the Surrealist Group, as Breton termed them.

Surrealism was in the first place a literary movement, as Dada had been. It drew heavily on two major sources: the new science of psychology and a Gothic/decadent tradition in French literature exemplified by the Comte de Lautréamont, whose obscure novel *Les Chants du Maldoror* expressed a morbid, sexually symbolic irrationality in startling imagery; 'as beautiful as the encounter on an operating table of a sewing machine and an umbrella' is an often-quoted line. Breton, who quickly established himself as the group's leader and chief spokesman (he was what would now be termed a 'control freak'), retrospectively identified a number of writers who had more or less conformed to the Surrealist ideal – de Sade, Verlaine, Rimbaud and others – claiming that their pursuits of liberation and truth had been harbingers of this modern crusade. He also saw himself as carrying on the spirit – or stepping into the shoes – of the great hero of the French avant-garde, Guillaume Apollinaire, the poet and critic who had died in the influenza epidemic of 1919. Thus, while Surrealism is often seen as the child of the Dada movement, the relationship was not as direct as the presence of so many ex-Dadaists in its ranks would suggest.

Miró had himself read Apollinaire while on military service in late 1917 or 1918, presumably on Picabia's recommendation. He was an avid reader, and often drew parallels between his painting and the art of writing poetry – indeed, the distinction between the two in some of his work is not great. Surrealism's literary bent would not have unsettled him; like Dada, the movement had few rules when it came to artistic production. The Surrealists concentrated on the creative process and its potential as a personally and socially liberating force; this would have appealed to Miró, who was fascinated by the 'force' which drove him to create. In any case it quickly became apparent that it was the painters who joined or followed the movement, rather than the poets, who captured the public's imagination.

In fact, it is clear that Masson and Miró were to some extent ahead of the game, and that far from introducing them to the possibilities of exploring their subconscious minds, they were already engaged in the process a year or more before Breton contacted Masson early in 1924. There had already been a certain exploration of that road within the Dada movement – for example, in the work of Hans Arp, which Miró would have known from the avant-garde journals he had seen at Dalmau's, and certainly among the Dada poets like Tzara. Irrationality is one of the chief links between Dadaism and Surrealism, the difference being that where Dada was content merely to be irrational, the Surrealists sought to harness and to justify irrationality. For Masson (in many ways a quintessential Surrealist) it meant a quest for automatism, for the abandonment of the senses – a very French and very literary concern inherited from the Symbolists, and in particular from Rimbaud. This led eventually to a long series of automatic drawings and paintings in which a rapidly, unthinkingly produced sinuous line is the starting point for images which redesign physical objects, in Breton's phrase, 'according to the laws of desire'. But for Miró, whose efforts until now had been in producing works of scrupulous precision, such abandonment was impossible. Instead his impulse took him in the opposite direction, toward the physical object first, subjecting reality to a kind of *mirada fuerte*, a gaze so intense that, as it were, the object was transformed into something which expressed not only its appearance but its significance – something more real, 'surreal'. This process can be seen clearly for the first time in *The Tilled Field* (1923, page 61).

The Tilled Field is essentially a revision of the mental and physical landscape first described in *The Kitchen Garden* and itemized in *The Farm*. The same creatures, now rendered for the most part in a style which distorts their physical appearance, inhabit the same yard with the same tree and the same farmhouse. As in *The Farmer's Wife*, the feet and legs of the aminals emphasize their contact with mother earth, while for the first time the schematic bird – which was to become a trademark of Miró's art – makes an appearance; the cockerel-like creature which flies in front of the cloud with a branch in its mouth (a Biblical reference?) is here at once bird and weather-vane. The tree has become a sort of guardian figure, possessing not only an eye but a huge ear, aware of everything around it. The bull – unmistakably a reference to prehistoric cave-painting, and thus to the immemoriality of the scene – pulls a plough which has changed the colour of both earth and sky. This is a device which harks back to *The Kitchen Garden* and which may also symbolize day turning into night and the passage of time in general. Just as in *The Kitchen Garden* Miró painted only sufficient grass around the donkey to show what he is eating, here he paints only a minimum of features needed to sum up each object. The prickly pear being eaten by the goat has only two huge leaves, each with one sharp edge. The mare has only three ribs, its foal four vertebrae. The fig-tree to the left has a single leaf on its snake-like branch, and a single fruit, and so on. Thus in attempting to summarize the features of physical objects – to produce the calligraphy of objects – Miró is moving toward the boundary between things and language. This quest was not at odds with the Surrealist programme, but it did mark him out as his own man.[29] In the paintings which followed *The Tilled Field* Miró rapidly formulated the language which distinguishes his mature work. By the end of 1923, when he was working on *Catalan Landscape (The Hunter)* the remaining traces of 'decadent' French art have been eliminated. *The Tilled Field* had used traditional perspective, albeit with the device of using a ruled 'floating' line for the horizon above the apparent horizon of the scene; in *The Hunter* this line is present but the organization of the objects in the picture makes little reference to it. All these objects have been reduced to constructions of lines and flat planes which hint at rather than describe their form. Dotted lines too suggest movement in a cartoon-like way. (Miró's immediate inspiration may have been the work of Paul Klee, whose famous dictum was that he was 'taking a line for a walk'.) Once again Miró is signifying objects by providing the minimum of visual information needed to identify them. The man is a not just a man (=ear, pipe) but a Catalan peasant (=hat) and a hunter (=gun). The animal has one rabbit's ear. Eventually Miró was to lose interest in providing even these scant clues.

This period in which he reuses the subjects of his detailist paintings in the search for a new formal language culminated in *The Carnival of Harlequin* (1924-25, page 71), a busy interior in which various previously used devices, such as the cockerel in the lower left corner, the huge ear (top left) and the eyes attached to inanimate objects, are combined with new ones. These include the ladder (a personal symbol of escape) and the fragment of a musical score to signify the sound of the guitar, which has a direct bearing on his interest in the relationship between things and language, that which is signified and that which signifies it. From here it is a logical step to painting sounds as well as visible objects. We also see that puzzling and apparently insignificant features of his previous pictures are repeated, implying an importance as private, personal symbols. In *The Hunter*, for example, in front of the rabbit's face is an insect from which four droplets of faeces are emanating, and this is repeated in *The Carnival of Harlequin*, on the moustache of the guitar-bodied pierrot. Likewise, more obvious obsessions are confirmed; the depiction of genital/anal hair in *The Hunter* is repeated in the cockerel-headed (but female) figure in *Harlequin*.

The Surrealist movement had officially been launched with the publication of its first manifesto in 1924. Miró had already met the three central figures Breton and his fellow poets Louis Aragon and Paul Eluard. The group launched its first periodical, *La Révolution Surréaliste*, in 1925, quarrelling with Picabia, who attacked them in *391* for abandoning Dada, which he saw as still having revolutionary potential. Miró was torn, and asked Masson whether he should throw his hat into the ring with Breton or stick with his old friend. Masson replied unhesitatingly that Breton was the man of the future, Picabia of the past.[30]

Miró was the first Surrealist to have a one-man show after the group's inception. The catalogue was written by the poet Benjamin Péret and the invitation signed by the whole group. The show, at Pierre Loeb's gallery, was a huge social event, with *le tout Paris* in attendance. It was the Surrealists, flavour of the month in the newspapers, who were the attraction rather than the unknown Catalan painter, and financially Miró gained little. For the group as a whole, however, it was a triumph, and Miró had the advantage of being the first 'name' associated with Surrealist art in the public mind. The first 'official' Surrealist exhibition was held in 1925, also at the Galerie Pierre, to which Miró contributed *The Carnival of Harlequin*. Picasso, Klee, Ernst, de Chirico, Man Ray and Arp were also included although, oddly, André Masson was not.

Surrealism was by far the most disparate movement, stylistically, in the history of art before or since; even Dada had had a certain uniformity of stylistic impoverishment. For the Surrealists style was not an important question; in their pursuit of 'the marvellous' only effect mattered. Aragon described Surrealist art as 'the uncontrolled and passionate use of the drug image'.[31] Of the exhibitors, Picasso was there as somewhat of an official blessing from on high; at this stage he was merely 'in the environs' of Surrealism, in Breton's phrase. De Chirico, the instigator of the Italian 'Metaphysical' school which was an important influence on Ernst, Dalí and the more 'representational' Surrealists, was also

there, as was Klee, whose concerns were strongly aesthetic and theoretical and rested on a quite different philosophical tradition. The closest in formal terms to Miró was Hans Arp, who became a close friend.

Arp had arrived at Surrealism via an exploration of the 'laws of chance'. This was a process with similarities to automatism, which he saw as bringing artistic production closer to the processes of nature, and via abstraction from natural forms. A gentle, thoughtful man, he had undergone a period of isolated closeness to nature similar to Miró's life at Montroig, and like Miró he was as interested in poetry as painting. Their humour too was on the same wavelength.

Miró had come to the end of his ideogrammatic revision of detailism. Immersed in the excitement of new debate and experiment, he began to explore the new visual logic suggested by Surrealism, though he chose to ignore the more literal tendency represented by Dalí, Ernst and Magritte. He also pursued his interest in the relationships between word and image, painting and poetry. In so doing he found that he was sharing the same philosophical ground as other artists, in particular, despite their very different styles, René Magritte.

Magritte's art is perhaps the purest form of Surrealism, in that it is less tainted by personal and tangential concerns than that of any other artist. His famous image of a tobacco pipe, labelled 'This is not a pipe' encapsulates his wish to force his audience into thinking about the relationship between words, visual objects and representation. The painting makes two points: firstly it is not a pipe but the image of a pipe, and secondly there is also the 'Surrealist question' is it a pipe at all? Is it perhaps a horse, or a cloud? In other words, what may be a pipe in the 'real world' may be something

---

Maternity 1924
Oil on canvas. 91 x 74 cm
National Gallery of Modern Art, Edinburgh

else in the world of dreams, of poetry, of the marvellous, the 'surreal world'. The two questions have further implications; if it is not a pipe but only a picture of a pipe, then this thing that is 'a picture of a pipe' may itself be something else. We are being warned to be on our guard – our whole world of appearances has been thrown into question, as if we are in a hall of mirrors. In other pictures he poses the same question in reverse, painting an object but calling it by an unfamiliar name.

Miró approaches these questions less directly, but his concerns are very largely the same. Between the winters of 1925 and 1927 he produced a series of 'dream paintings' (a somewhat misleading label), typified by monochromatic backgrounds on which areas of colour, some 'biomorphic', some geometric, are placed (*Painting*, 1926, page 81 and *The Siesta*, 1925, page 77). Into these he began to incorporate letters and fragments of words, or calligraphic signs which suggest words but often do not 'mean' anything interpretable. He produced scores of these images in what was for him an unprecedented burst of creative energy. Unlike Masson and other members of the group, however, these were not 'automatic' images, and neither were they abstract. The starting points were always actual physical things: cracks in the wall, a passage he had read, a cloud.[32] The images were very deliberately composed, in the sense that a poem is composed. Some, like *The Siesta*, are interpretable as landscapes with figures; others are collections of 'free-floating' forms (*Painting*, page 81). Miró never 'abandoned' himself in their production; his work ethic, his sense of craft, remained intact. This was one of the things which caused him to drift gradually away from the centre of the Surrealist movement. He was too much his own man, and his methods were too deliberate, to endear him to Breton, despite his 'sound' motivation. Breton, whose authoritarian streak rapidly alienated many of the group, made the often-quoted observation that 'Miró may be the most surrealist of all of us'. Sometimes taken as unqualified approval, it was in fact an ironic aside: Breton is acknowledging that Miró remained something of a closed book, and therefore outside 'official' control.

Despite the decline of Picabia's star, it was to Dada that Miró turned in his search for a way to incorporate his recent innovations into the Surrealist programme. The incorporation of words and letters into the dream images had produced what he termed 'poem-paintings' (*Oh! Un de ces messieurs qui a fait tout ça*, 1925, page 75), and these led logically into 'poem-objects', in which discovered objects are incorporated into the image. Both traits have their ancestry in the art of international Dada during the war; the art of Picabia, Duchamp and their followers. It would have been apparent in retrospect that when Picabia took a mechanical diagram and labelled it 'Nude' he was challenging traditional visual logic, the power of language and the bourgeois values which traditional art upheld. All that had changed was that the anti-philosophy of Dada had been developed, amplified and given structure. Picabia saw this as a betrayal of liberty, the onset of a new and authoritarian bureaucracy. (It was no accident that Breton had set up a 'Bureau of Surrealist Enquiries', or that in the 1930s the Surrealists were 'officially' aligned to the most illiberal bureaucracy of all, that of the Communist Party.) Miró, however, saw no reason not to borrow from Dada, and in images such as the quintessential 'poem-painting' *This Is the Colour of My Dreams* (1925, page 79) to go so far as to blur the distinction between the title of the painting (its name being what it is) and the painting itself, and to play a purely Dadaist joke by labelling it 'Photo'. In this work he anticipates Magritte's *This is not a pipe* by a year. It may be that Magritte's inspiration, and thus a whole canon of later Surrealism, came from Miró's work rather than directly from Dada, in which Magritte had not been involved.[33]

A project which did nothing to endear Miró to Breton was his acceptance in 1926 with Max Ernst of a commission to design the sets and costumes of the Ballets Russes production of *Romeo and Juliet*. Not only was the ballet in Breton's eyes a dangerously bourgeois art-form but the production itself was of the most cliché-ridden and banal of all love-stories. When in 1928 Breton published his treatise *Surrealism and Painting* he called on artists to rely wholly on an 'interior model'.

Miró's insistence on always starting from an exterior object thus put him outside the most rigorous definition of the movement, though he continued to be closely associated with it. Like Picasso Miró managed to maintain a dignified, somewhat patrician distance from the centre of the group. They claimed him; he did not claim to be one of them.

Despite his initial close involvement, Miró cared little for Breton's politicking. As with Dada, he was content to learn what he could, to take what was useful, but nothing would persuade him to give up the sovereignty of his own art. He continued to retreat from Paris every summer (another sin according to Breton, Aragon and Eluard) to Montroig. Another factor in his relationship with the Surrealists may have been his age: Miró was thirty-four in 1927, and had been a full-time painter for over sixteen years. He was thus a good deal older than most of the budding Surrealists, and no doubt less impressionable and more self-confident, besides being set in his ways.

Miró's father died in 1926, though what the son's feelings were at this event we do not know. From this time his art moved away from the poem-objects and poem-paintings and began once again to refer to landscapes and interiors, often reintroducing signs and objects which have their origins in his detailist period (*Landscape with Cockerel*, 1927, page 85). His colours reintensified, and he began to experiment with different materials, using collages and discovered objects and painting on surfaces such as glasspaper and masonite. He continued to work hard, producing fourteen canvases on each of his Montroig visits in 1926 and 1927[34]; these works were laboriously created, and it was his dedication and long hours in the studio, rather than speed of execution, which made him so productive.

There were signs that his reputation was growing; two of his paintings were shown at the International Modern Art exhibition in Brooklyn in 1926, and his sales (he was represented chiefly by Pierre Loeb) were beginning to accelerate. In 1927 he moved out of Gargallo's rue

Blomet studio and took one at the heart of the Parisian scene, in the rue Tourlaque, Montmartre, where his neighbours included Ernst, Arp and Magritte, all expatriates. All were also somewhat sceptical in their attitude to Breton. Miró had other things in common with each of them. Ernst had a similar fixation with birds and enigmatic female figures, and with his own past and childhood, and was also interested in experimental techniques. Magritte shared Miró's playful attitude to the philosophy and language of signs, and was a scrupulously orderly, sober and conservatively dressed man whose 'bourgeois' appearance concealed a fine sense of humour. Arp and Miró shared a love of nature, a symbolic language (stars, flowers, birds, 'personages') and, to some extent, a formal language. This now grew even closer; Miró's *Construction* (1930, page 93) could pass as Arp's work. Likewise many of Miró's titles and painted inscriptions are close to Arp's language. 'We shared', he remembered, 'each other's poverty and radishes'[35] – perhaps a reference to the organic, vegetable-like forms that united their art.

In 1928 Miró, perhaps at Magritte's suggestion, made a visit to Belgium and the Netherlands, the result of which was several works which have as their starting points seventeenth-century Dutch paintings. The first (*Dutch Interior I*, 1928) was a revision of *The Lutanist* (1661) by Hendrick Martensz Sorgh, which he saw at the Rijksmuseum, Amsterdam. Working from a postcard reproduction back in Paris, Miró gradually worked-over each element in the picture, sketching and re-sketching, subjecting them one by one to his *mirada fuerte*, arriving finally at something on the borders between comedy and nightmare, both playful and disturbing. In the second (*Dutch Interior II*, 1928, page 87), based on Jan Steen's *The Cat's Dancing Lesson*, the 'dancing' cat and musician are welded together with a pipe-smoking onlooker, while another figure has been reduced to a gigantic head and two encircling arms, which are squeezing a dog like a balloon. Miró's short series of revisions continued with a further *Dutch Interior* and four 'imaginary portraits', beginning with *Portrait of Mrs Mills in 1750* (1929, page 91) based on the work of the English miniaturist George Engleheart. In these the forms, and the pictorial space, have been considerably flattened from those in the Dutch series, and a more playful, writerly line is apparent. While these pictures cannot in any sense be described as being based on an 'interior model', they do undoubtedly conform to the Surrealist ethic, and thus point out the restrictive nature of Breton's critique. Indeed, one can argue that while their effect and style are surreal, their inspiration is Dadaist – a playful yet savage attack on traditional decorative art, calculated to offend. It is interesting that Miró should for the time being have abandoned his usual 'internal landscape', his *enyoranca*. He was never to do so again.

In 1928 Miró held a successful one-man show at the Galerie Georges Bernheim in Paris. Although he was not yet financially secure (and would not be until after the Second World War), his international reputation began to flourish, particularly in America. In that year he also made a trip to Madrid, visiting the Prado for the first time, and then journeyed to Mallorca which he held in almost as great an affection as Montroig. It was in Mallorca that he met Pilar Juncosa, whom he married the following year in Palma. They settled in Paris, and in 1931 had a daughter, Maria Dolores.

Miró's painting was by now settled into three broad categories, between which he switched. Firstly were what may loosely be called 'landscapes', usually featuring forms reminiscent of humans and animals and a horizon to suggest perspective (*Landscape with Cockerel*, 1927, page 85). In the second category were 'interiors' in which these signs are situated in an enclosed space (which might of course be 'metaphysical' – for example, *Queen Louise of Prussia,* 1929, page 89). The third group consisted of paintings in which these forms 'float' freely when placed on a uniform background with, depending on how they are read, either little or no sense of depth or an infinite space (*Painting*, 1933, page 97). These approaches, combined with his experimentation with materials, provided for an almost infinite variety; within them Miró was always developing new symbolic configurations, reworking previous formulae in new ways, always allowing himself to be influenced by what he found valuable in the outside world. The influences of other artists (around this time Arp and Klee, for example; later Picasso, in the 1950s the Abstract Expressionists, in the 1960s Pop Art) are from time to time very strong, but Miró always manages to transform these sources for his own purposes. Essentially, all his painting after about 1930 falls into these three categories, but having established them, he underwent the first of what were to become quite frequent and prolonged periods during which for various reasons he turned to other means of expression.

At the beginning of the 1930s Miró seems to have become disillusioned with traditional painting, and for the next two years the majority of his productions were drawings, constructions, paintings on experimental surfaces and, in particular, collages. At Montroig in the summer of 1932 he made twelve small pictures on wood, based on the female form; these marked the beginning of the transformation of Woman in his pictures from a specific role (the Catalan farmer's wife, the bourgeoise Mrs Mills) to a universal one. It is difficult not to draw a parallel between the beginning of this process – in which the woman-figure in his painting is made, over the years, sometimes hideously threatening and predatory and at other times serene and benign – and the artist's marriage. Certainly it would be easy to make a case, as many critics have done (based on Miró's imagery of the 1930s and 1940s) that he was a hopeless misogynist, terrified of female sexual power. This, however, is not a conclusion one should jump to, and those who have done so have perhaps been seduced by apparent similarities between the distortions of the female figure in Miró's work and in that of Pablo Picasso. The two men, however, were very different. Miró was never a Lothario, nor was he an egotist who needed women to reassure him of his masculinity. His marriage was one of lifelong contentment. Whereas in Picasso's work the female figure can all too often be related to his feelings for one or other of his endless succession of lovers, in Miró's paintings women never relate to specific

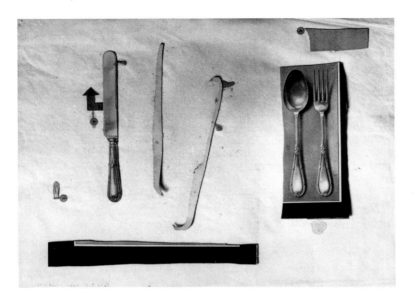

Preparatory Collage for Painting *1933*
Pencil and collage on paper. 47.1 x 63.1 cm
Fundacio Miró, Barcelona

---

individuals. They are ciphers, not just of women in general, but often of wider 'female' forces: the sea, the earth, Spain, Cataluña, 'Mother Nature', the Fates. While his sexuality, and 'the sexual' in general, are a major force in his art, his sex life is not. His paintings are littered with phallic and, in particular, with vaginal signs, and with breasts, mouths, armpits, pubic hair. He saw sex as a primal force and, like blood and excrement and death, he felt it to be an inescapable part of the natural energy which drove him, and which his art attempts to describe. One has to admit that he frequently produced images, particularly in the period of the Spanish Civil War and through the Second World War, in which the female and female sexuality are very specifically expressive of horror and loathing. On the other hand this must be balanced by the historical context of his work; he was after all born into a conservative stratum of one of the most macho of all European cultures, and his adult cultural milieu, the Surrealist movement, constituted at times little more than a concerted male assault on the 'mystery' of female sexual psychology. Miró himself would not be drawn on the subject, except to resist the suggestion that his own sexuality was a prime motivator.

The 1930s saw the increazing politicization of the Surrealist movement and of Miró himself in the face of the rise of Fascism. With the magazine *La Revolution Surréaliste* rechristened *Le Surréalisme au service de la Révolution*, Miró found himself further distanced from the centre of the movement. Surrealist artists and poets joined cells of communist workers in the factories and offices of Paris and the movement began to indulge in arguments with the Party, which saw Surrealism as an élitist intellectual diversion, tainted by the capitalist art market. In so far as he was political at all, Miró was sympathetic to the Left, but had no intention of joining the Party or of permitting political dogma to delimit his art. He was, however, filled with a growing sense of foreboding about the turn of political events, particularly in Spain. 'I had this unconscious feeling of impending disaster. The feeling you have before it starts to rain, with aching limbs and a stifling numbness. It was a physical rather than a psychological sensation. I had a premonition that there would soon be a catastrophe, though I did not know [what it would be]'[36]. This unease coincided with both the political upheavals within the Surrealist group and with his abandonment of conventional painting, which can be seen as a reaction to these crises.

Typically, Miró sought reassurance by turning to a mental, disciplinary challenge. He began to make works from collaged elements – pictures taken from newspapers and magazines, which he arranged and reshuffled on plain white paper for long, thoughtful periods before anchoring them. These then became the starting points of a long series of sketches as, in the same way that the elements of the Dutch paintings had been transformed, the 'found' pictures were metamorphosed into new forms. His sketchbooks speak of the immense concentration and energy he expended in this process – painting was no longer easy for him, because he was energized not by the 'telluric' force he drew from nature but by the unease and anxiety of the times.

Throughout his life Miró was prone to fits of depression and violent emotion, though in public he was always

Nude Descending a Staircase No 2
by Marcel Duchamp 1920
Oil on canvas. 147.3 x 88.9 cm
Philadelphia Museum of Art

urbane and quiet. The dominant side of his nature, however, was the humorous, serene one, and he was always able to produce playful, light-hearted works such as the little collage-drawing *Homage to Prats* (1934, page 99), a reference to his closest friend since their days at the Cercle Artistic de Sant Lluc, now running a hatter's shop in Barcelona. When Miró did

return to painting he launched himself into what he called his 'savage paintings', often using materials like sandpaper instead of canvas, in which his pictorial language loses its grace and previously sinuous forms are twisted into tortured new shapes. This series grew out of a number of pastel drawings made in the summer of 1934 (*Woman*, page 101).

In 1932 Miró had moved with his family back to Barcelona to live with his widowed mother in the flat in the Passatge del Credit. He was almost unknown in his own country, although his reputation in France was well established (at least among the intelligentsia), and his international one growing, with exhibitions in Brussels and New York in 1930 and Chicago in 1931 as well as Surrealist Group shows. Increasingly he was alienated ideologically from the Surrealists, though still on cordial terms with them, and Paris no longer had much appeal for him. He was still very much a Catalan.

Inevitably, the political situation in Spain began to affect him more and more. Spending long periods in the quiet of Montroig, he realized vividly what his country stood to lose in its descent toward civil war. From this point his work is often painted in lurid, acid colours, full of monstrous beings, male and female, with reptilian, fanged jaws, and genitalia resembling spiked weapons or clawed traps. At other times events conspired to produce more gentle and poetic works; in 1932 he designed his second ballet, *Jeux d'enfants*, for the Ballets Russes of Monte Carlo, a production which travelled to Barcelona in the following year. He met Wassily Kandinsky, whose abstract colour compositions he had long admired, and Paul Klee, whose gentle pictographic style produces a new lyricism in his own work (*Snail, Woman, Flower, Star*, 1934; *Swallow of Love*, 1934). All three shared a view of art as searching for a synthesis of word, sound, colour and image.

By the mid-1930s, Miró's paintings are almost universally pessimistic. The 'savage paintings' (such as *Personages in the Presence of a Metamorphosis*, 1936) give way to scenes which in their concentration on the metamorphosis of human forms into mutant assemblages of organs and limbs are reminiscent of the response of Salvador Dalí to the horrors of the times. This remains true despite their opposed political views. Ironically, by July 1936, when the crisis in Spain erupted into all-out war, Miró had become a major international figure, with exhibition in London, Paris, Lucerne, Copenhagen and New York, where since 1932 he had been represented by a leading dealer, Pierre Matisse. Miró's American reputation was sealed by his inclusion in one of the most influential exhibitions of the 1930s, the huge *Fantastic Art, Dada, Surrealism* show at New York's Museum of Modern Art in 1936. This made the reputations of the Surrealists in the USA (particularly that of Dalí, anagrammatically nicknamed 'Avida Dollars' by his now bitter enemies on the Left).

At the outbreak of the Spanish Civil War Miró was in London; he went from there to Paris, where his family joined him in November. Paris was already filling with refugees from Hitler's Germany, as well as from Spain, and among the artistic community an atmosphere of feverish political debate reigned. Miró accepted a commission (*The Reaper*, now lost) for the Republican pavilion at the 1937 Universal Exhibition in Paris, in which building Picasso displayed his *Guernica*. He also designed the poster *Aidez l'Espagne!* (page 103), included in an edition of *Cahiers d'Art* dedicated to Spanish painting in aid of the Republican forces.

The series of metamorphic paintings culminated in a unique work in Miró's œuvre, *Still Life with Old Shoe* (1937), in which a number of everyday objects are assembled on a table – a bottle, a loaf, a fork, a fig and a shoe – and shown in a comparatively realistic style, only gently distorted. Once again the closest formal parallel is with Dalí, but this is probably coincidental. Here, instead of the hallucinatory clarity of Dalí we have a brooding, lurid scene in which acid green, blue, yellow and scarlet are played off against a black background, as if the objects are rotting and giving off a phosphorescent glow as they decompose. It is an eloquent expression of Miró's despair at the savagery

being forced on his country and what he felt to be its magical and sacred peasant culture. However, he said that at the time he was 'not aware that I was painting my *Guernica*', just that 'somehow I wanted to capture those dramatic and sad times'.[37]

Perhaps because of the hopelessness of the situation in Spain, Miró's most pessimistic period – which culminated in 1938 with a series of horrific and bitterly ironic canvases in which female figures become either monstrous reptiles (*Decoration for a Nursery*, 1938) or wrinkled hags (*Seated Woman II*, 1938) – suddenly gave way to a flood of lyrical poeticism, even whimsy,

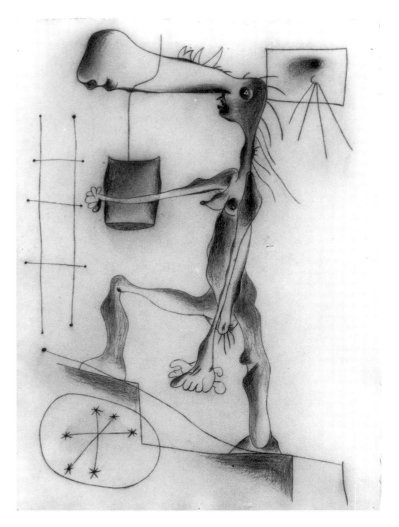

Nude Woman Climbing a Staircase *1937*
Pencil on paper. 78 x 50 cm
Fundacio Miró, Barcelona

which was to last until the end of the Second World War. But then he had always had reserves of inner strength which kept the darker side of his nature in check. As he remarked of another painting full of the atmosphere of the war, *Man and Woman in Front of a Heap of Excrement* (1937), 'I was fascinated by Rembrandt's words: "I can find rubies and emeralds in a pile of dung".'[38] Around this time he painted a provocative response to a work by his fellow exhibitor at Dalmaus, Marcel Duchamp, countering Duchamp's *Nude Descending a Staircase Nº 2* with *Nude Woman Climbing a Staircase*. In fact Miró appears to have admired Duchamp, apparently keeping the gift of a tie for over 50 years.

In the summer of 1939 Miró and his family rented a house in the village of Varengeville-sur-Mer, Normandy, close to the home of Georges Braque, who was a close friend despite not being part of the Surrealist circle. Miró had visited Varengeville previously, impressed by the unfamiliar northern light and Atlantic climate, but when the war came he withdrew there with his few possessions and his family, hoping to weather the storm.

His works are henceforth marked by two new factors: an increasing scarcity of materials (not so much of a hardship for one so used to experimentation) and a new interconnection of forms inspired, he said, by his love of music, making the picture surface an arena on which lines, characters and colours can be read like the passage of a series of sounds. An early example of the Varengeville series is *A Drop of Dew Falling from the Wing of a Bird Wakes Rosalie from her Sleep in the Shadow of a Spider's Web* (1939, page 109) in which both factors are visible – it is painted on sackcloth. He also worked on a long series of drawings (on scrap paper) which were intended, should the opportunity arise, to form the basis of a set of lithographs.

But the most important development of this period is the series called *Constellations* (page 111), begun on 20th January 1940, with *The Sunrise*. It is immediately apparent that Miró's personal repertoire of symbols

and personages have here been bound together in a kind of network – reminiscent of the diagrams of heavenly constellations – which is suggestive of a musical score and which appears to stress the interconnectedness not just of natural objects but of the physical and spiritual worlds. Music, which Miró uses as a metaphor for the spiritual, is here physically tied to forms, so that the outlines of bodies become musical 'phrases', emphasizing this interrelation. The war had forced Miró from the critical, 'paranoid' position of his 'savage paintings' into a determination to set down what he saw as fundamental values and poetic truths. The direct formal inspiration must have been the work of Paul Klee, which Miró had occasionally seen in Paris but which he had been shown secretly by a dealer in Berlin (Klee had been marked down by the Nazis as a 'degenerate artist'). The *Constellations* are not a retreat from the oncoming shadow of Nazism, but the boldest possible statement of defiance, using the only weapon at his disposal. Their production was immensely difficult. Miró prepared paper by scraping the surface gently and colouring it with pallid wash, sometimes also using charcoal and crayon or pastel. This produced diffused forms – he compared the inspiration to the reflections of objects in moving water. He then made rapid, free-flowing sketches separately, working these up until he was satisfied with the composition. The image was then copied with absolute fidelity from the drawing, using gouache. Each took up to a month to complete, and there are twenty-three in all.

By 1940, with about ten of the *Constellations* series completed, the German advance persuaded Miró that he would be better off in his home country, which though already under Fascist rule was at least relatively tranquil. He returned to Paris and managed to get his family on to the last train south. At first they stayed in the family flat but he was told by friends that he would not be safe in Barcelona, and he moved on to Mallorca, out of sight and out of mind of Franco's regime. Although he showed work in Barcelona from 1960, his first Madrid exhibition was not until 1976, after Franco's death. In Mallorca he took up the *Constellations* series once

Stage set for the ballet Jeux d'enfants *1932*
Fundacio Miró, Barcelona

again, and when that was complete he produced further works on paper: this was a period which seems as much to do with his own uncertainty about painting as with the scarcity of paint and canvas. But in 1942 his mother's age and infirmity made him go back to his parents' house in the Passatge del Credit, Barcelona.

Miró's sign language developed significantly during the war, as he honed his personal symbols, repeating them again and again in new configurations, attempting to draw from them every nuance of magic and poetic expression. His concentration on graphic work was doubtless important in this process. These symbols become fluid calligraphic signs, as natural to his hand as the letters of his own signature, graceful, poised. Woman is almost omnipresent, very often in a night-time setting surely symbolic of the war; her companions are the stars, symbols of hope and aspiration; birds, representing spirituality and freedom; and very often the ladder, his 'escape ladder' which connects the Earth with the heavens, his route from reality into the imagination, from imprisonment into freedom. His pictures continue to maintain their mood of quiet optimism in the face of darkness, perfectly expressed by titles such as *The Nightingale's Song at Midnight and the Morning Rain*, and *Personages in the Night Guided by the Phosphorescent Tracks of Snails*. Miró's personages and animals are as much hidden and protected as they are threatened by the night.

During the war years, no new work found its way out of Spain to the wider world, but unknown to Miró an

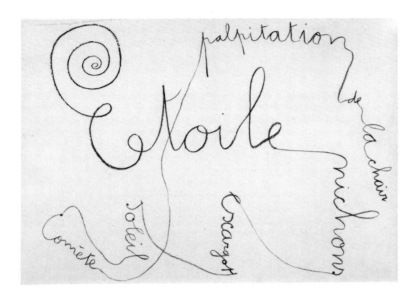

Etoiles, Nichons, Escargots 1937
Poem drawing. 75 x 105 cm
Musée National d'Art Moderne, Paris

event was taking place in the USA which was to lay the foundation of his post-war status as one of the few artists to enjoy a truly international reputation. In 1941 James Johnson Sweeney organized a Miró retrospective at the Museum of Modern Art, which was an enormous critical and public success. With a very large proportion of Europe's artistic community now exiled in America – not only painters and sculptors but teachers, critics and dealers – Miró's work (which included paintings and constructions, drawings, prints, etchings, stage designs and even tapestry) was presented to perhaps the greatest concentration of artistic talent and influence ever assembled in one country. The consequences of the exhibition were profound, not just for his post-war career, but for the effect his work had on a generation of American painters – Arshile Gorky, Jackson Pollock, Clyfford Still, Sam Francis, Adolph Gottlieb – who were, as the 'Abstract Expressionists', to form the vanguard of modernism in the late 1940s and 1950s.

With the tide of the war turning, Miró began to return to larger, more permanent works, and embarked on the first of many collaborations with his old friend, Llorens

Artigas, now a professional potter and ceramicist. Artigas had a studio in Barcelona, and Miró became fascinated by a heap of broken pieces (the result of a misfiring of the kiln) which Artigas had been intending to sweep up. Instead Miró decorated them with enamel, using their distorted shapes to suggest painted forms and lines, and they were refired. *Ceramic Plaque* (1946, page 115) marked the beginning of a collaboration which was to be at least as important as painting to Miró for the next thirty years. He also completed the fifty lithographs from the series of drawings made in 1939 at Varengeville, which became known as the *Barcelona* series.

As the war drew to an end Miró's American reputation received a further boost with an exhibition, the first new work by a European artist since 1939, of the *Constellations* series at the Pierre Matisse Gallery in January 1945. Miró's colourful lyricism seemed perfectly in tune with the optimism of the time. The new ceramics were also included.

The end of the war marks the end also of the undercurrent of anxiety in Miró's work. Although he was never entirely at ease with himself, and still prone to periods of introspective gloom, the immediate post-war years see the expression of a new simplicity and *joie de vivre* in his work. It would be untrue to say that his paintings were never again touched by violence or anger – in fact, violence or anger are on occasion more forcefully present than ever before – but these destructive forces tend to find expression in his modus operandi, in technical rather than iconographic distortions. For the time being he returned to painting on canvas in a series whose titles – *Hope* (1946), *Woman and Birds at Sunrise* (1946) – mark the end of the night.

Pierre Matisse arranged the commission of a mural for the restaurant of the Cincinnati Plaza Terrace Hotel, and in 1947 Miró took his family to New York for the first time. 'I didn't much like the idea of my work hanging in a restaurant', he said later, 'but Pierre assured me that it would end up in the Cincinnati Art Museum, and it did.'[39] Between February and October, Miró worked at a canvas ten metres in length and three in height. His painting ushers in the post-war phenomemon of the wall-sized canvas, and his art, with its rich, saturated colour and generous, expressive line, was perfectly suited to this scale. During his stay he met the chief theoretician of Abstract Expressionism, Clement Greenberg, and its *enfant terrible*, Jackson Pollock.

He fell in love with the USA, and returned there many times. He loved jazz, and made a pilgrimage to Harlem with his friend the sculptor Alexander Calder and his wife. In Harlem, he liked to recall, he was invited to dance by a very tall black woman, who towered above him and engulfed his short, compact figure. (Miró had always been an enthusiastic dancer, and had been noted in Paris for his mastery of the tango. The solemn passion and slight absurdity of the dance appealed to the Surrealists and perfectly expressed their – and his – combination of humour and sexual passion.)

On his return to Europe, Miró was sufficiently encouraged by his American experience to work on another mural, this time painting directly on to fibrocement, a process which he had first tried during the experimental phase of the late 1930s (*Mural Painting for Joaquim Gomis*, 1947). He moved back to Paris, working on large canvases which tend to describe single monumental 'personages' created by almost 'gestural' calligraphy and filled with large areas of unmodulated colour, accompanied by a limited 'setting' of symbols or signs which are sometimes contrastingly exact in execution. The sexuality of his figures again becomes more overt (*The Red Sun Gnaws at the Spider*, 1948).

A large-scale exhibition of his work in 1948 at the Galerie Maeght in Paris, and subsequently in New York, confirmed his new status as an international superstar of art, and his painting became prolific – fifty-five canvases in the year 1949-50, sixty in 1952-53, plus innumerable drawings and increasing numbers of sculptures, ceramics and lithographs. He was awarded the Grand Prize at the 1954 Venice Biennale for his

graphic work. A great deal of his time henceforth was taken up by projects in other media, particularly ceramics, and when he did return to painting it was often to try to bring to it something which he had learned from this wider experience.

Miró's partnership with Llorens Artigas was one of the closest and most fruitful of any in modern art, and Artigas is rarely given sufficient credit for his contribution. Initially, he simply produced objects – tiles, jugs, vases – to Miró's specifications, which the painter would then decorate. Over the years this collaboration deepened, however, as Miró received more and more commissions for ceramic and sculptural work. Artigas was not only responsible for the technical decisions which enabled Miró to realize his plans; they knew each other so well that the ceramicist was often able to suggest techniques which he realized would contribute to the artist's means of expression, thus directly influencing the works themselves.

Artigas now lived in the remote mountain village of Gallifa with his son, who acted as an assistant in the studio. Gallifa took the place in the 1950s and 1960s

Verso of the plate The Morning Star
from Constellations New York 1959
Dept. des Imprimés, Bibliothèque Nationale, Paris

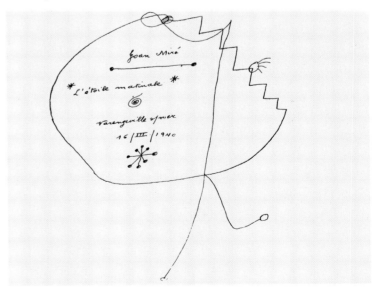

that Montroig had filled in the pre-war years. There was no telephone there and the quiet and simplicity of the village, the rugged scenery and intense, pure light, were a source of spiritual renewal for Miró.

Another old friend, the architect Josep Lluis Sert, was now teaching at Harvard University in Massachusetts, under the distinguished founder of the Bauhaus, Walter Gropius. They arranged Miró's second big project in the USA, a mural for the university's Graduate Center. Executed in Paris, the work was exhibited there and in New York before installation. In the following year (1952) Miró saw a large exhibition in Paris of Jackson Pollock's work, and for the first time began to approach his own canvases directly, without making any preparatory sketches or drawings. This re-energized his work for a time, but without developing his painterly language any further.

Although his painting of this period (1948-52) represents to many the 'classic' Miró – in the sense that it achieves a new grandeur of scale and a supreme confidence of execution – it was really the summing-up of the phase that had begun in the late 1930s and had moved through the periods of the 'savage paintings' and the *Constellations*. One of the results was a very large canvas (two metres by four) commissioned by the Guggenheim Foundation. It is noticeable that exposure to American painting often precipitated new bursts of creativity in Miró. He found that its directness and spontaneity added something to his quest (begun so long ago at Montroig) for the 'calligraphy' of everyday things, something which his own methodical and cautious approach had denied to him. But this new energy did not make its mark for long. Masterly though they are (for example, *The Eagle Flies to the Mountain Peaks Hollowed Out By Comets to Announce the Words of the Poet*, 1953, page 119), many of the works of the early 1950s have lost the passion which marks his best work of the previous years, and he again drifted away from the easel for a time.

One impetus of this period of reappraisal was his

Poster for the exhibition at the Maeght Gallery, 1948
Colour lithograph 65 x 50 cm
Fundacio Miró, Barcelona

decision to move permanently to Mallorca. Miró's recognition had come late – he was sixty years old in 1953 – and now financially secure he felt it was time to end his peripatetic existence. He commissioned Sert to design him a villa and a big, airy studio – he had as far back as 1932 written an article entitled 'I dream of a large studio', in which he also talked of a desire to explore new media.[40] The villa, called Son Abrines, was discussed and designed from 1954, but Miró didn't move in until 1956. The flat in Barcelona was put up for sale, and the accumulation of forty years of productive work had to be sorted and moved from there and from Paris. This process came at an ideal time, giving him the opportunity to stand back and assess his work, to mark or even rediscover aspects which he felt could be of use in future projects, and to arrive at a clearer idea of the direction of that future. 'I corrected myself coldly and objectively...I was pitiless with myself. I destroyed an enormous number of canvases, and especially drawings and gouaches'[41].

One of the differences between successful and unknown artists, however, is that the former may find that the demands of others govern their production to a greater extent. Increasingly Miró devoted his time to big, prestigious projects. One of the largest was a commission in 1955 to decorate two enormous walls at the new UNESCO building in Paris. He had done little painting since 1952, apart from a series of small works on cardboard, and decided to create twin ceramic tile murals (*Wall of the Sun* and *Wall of the Moon*, 1957-58). It was a project which appealed to him immensely; he had remarked in the article 'I dream of a large studio' that he felt that easel painting's aims were in the end 'rather petty' and that he was searching for an art which was 'closer to the masses of humanity, of whom I never cease to think'[42]. The large-scale mural, tapestry or sculpture was thus to him the end of art, a public rather than private thing. For inspiration he and Artigas went to visit the prehistoric cave-paintings at Altamira, an interest first evidenced in *The Tilled Field* over thirty years previously.

At first the new studio rather frightened him. It was very big indeed – sixty feet long – and had a sterile atmosphere. Even the vast amount of material which he had brought with him made little impression on it. Gradually, however, it began to fill with new creations and with things brought in from the outside world – boulders, branches and logs, terracotta figures, pots, pumpkins, old implements – until it became, in his words, 'like a forest'. Not that it was chaotic – Miró was obsessively orderly – but after years of working in small studios and the spare rooms of flats, its cavernous, cool space needed filling up. When the artist and critic Walter Erben visited him there in the 1950s he found

to his surprise that what he took to be work in progress – an arrangement of signs painted on papers weighed down with stones on the floor – was in fact gathering dust, having been placed there some years earlier. Miró would carefully move a piece from time to time, searching for the right composition. But he hadn't found it yet.[43] In contrast, he told Rosamond Bernier that in the privacy of his studio he went 'completely wild. The older I get, the meaner and more aggressive I get.'[44] Even in his late sixties, Miró worked to a punishing schedule, alone for long hours, in silence; visitors were absolutely forbidden. The studio, which had a terrace giving an uninterrupted view of the hilly Mallorcan interior, was placed at the end of the garden, separated from it by a high wall with a gate. But while he worked the windows were shuttered.

In 1959 Miró travelled to the USA on the occasion of a retrospective held in New York and Los Angeles, and to receive the Grand Prix of the Guggenheim Foundation for his UNESCO murals, presented to him on May 18th by President Eisenhower. Here he gained a second commission from Harvard University, and again he chose to work with Llorens Artigas on a ceramic mural, which was exhibited the following year in Barcelona, Paris and New York before installation.

Once again American art caused a new creative urgency in his work. Abstract Expressionism had moved from its 'gestural', 'action art' phase into a calm, grandiose maturity; exemplified by the 'colour field' work of Barnett Newman, Clyfford Still, Helen Frankenthaler and Morris Louis. Miró, excited by the enormous scale and glowing colours of these pictures (which he saw again in 1961) began to work on similarly large and simple canvases. The culmination of these was the series *Blue I, II, III* (1961), in each of which a vast area (the pictures are all 270 x 355 cm) of limpid sky-blue is interrupted only by small, rotund forms in black and single patches of red. These are serene pictures, the most purely spiritual, and most abstract, of all Miró's works. The effect is of a Zen-like combination of simplicity and humour, but above all a sense of weightlessness and limitless space. In other works, however, the influence seems to be that of Pollock or de Kooning; the image is rendered with a new restlessness, the hitherto precise lines smudged and scratched, splashes of paint dripped onto the canvas, or a few simple brushstrokes defining one of his private cosmology of signs (*Personage*, 1960, page 123) Between these two tendencies we can perhaps glimpse the two sides of his nature, the ascetic, orderly craftsman observed by Erben and the 'wild, mean' artist he professed himself to be to Bernier.

1962 saw an exhibition of 250 of his works at the Musée Nationale d'Art Moderne in Paris, while in Spain, after the Grand Prix at Venice, Miró became better known: one of the reasons for his move to Mallorca was that he resented the increased attention and demands on his time in Barcelona. He was still *persona non grata* with the Franco government and therefore with the official art world of museums, universities, art schools and galleries too. Barcelona's tradition of opposition to the capital Madrid, however, ensured that in his home town his reputation was secure, and in 1962 a Joan Miró Prize for Drawing was created there.

Miró's prodigious work-rate showed no signs of slowing as he entered his seventies. Big international projects continued to occupy him, but alongside these he produced large quantities of work in other media. His work as a monumental sculptor came to be increasingly in demand as the 1960s drew on. The inauguration of the Maeght Foundation at Saint-Paul-de-Vence in 1964 brought a commission for a maze (which he peopled with his sculptures), and he produced another ceramic mural with Artigas, in St Gall, Switzerland. That year also saw his first major retrospective in Britain, at the Tate Gallery. At the other end of the artistic scale, he produced a cover for the Catalan children's magazine *Cavall Fort* in 1965. A year later he and Artigas were working together again, on an underwater sculpture, *Venus of the Sea*, at Juan-les-Pins on the Riviera.

Miró had long been interested in oriental culture, and in 1966 he travelled to Japan for a retrospective of his work in Tokyo and Kyoto. Always open to influences, his paintings in the mid-sixties often have an oriental look, due partly to their calligraphic forms but also to their contemplative, spare distribution of masses (*The Smile of the Star to the Twin Tree of the Plain*, 1968, page 131; *Untitled*, 1967, page 125). As before, his style appears to change rapidly, and there are works in which the intensity of colour and complications of form are as striking as they had been twenty years before. One of the reasons for this was undoubtedly that he tended to put paintings aside for long periods – often years – until the mood took him to continue or rework them. Many of the canvases therefore have their starting points years before the dates which are traditionally assigned to them.

Miró's work also continued to reflect the wider world of modern art throughout this period. The work of Jasper Johns is strongly recalled in paintings of the late 1960s which use stencilled lettering; words and letters are of course commonplace in his work in various periods, but here he sometimes uses them for their formal rather than their poetic value (*Letters and Numbers Attracted by a Spark I*, 1968). Miró's sculpture too sometimes seems to acknowledge Pop Art, with the inclusion of, for instance, the shapely legs of a shop-window mannequin (painted an outrageous lipstick pink) in *Fleeing Young Girl*, 1968. His interest in tapestry and the textural possibilities it offered resulted in a number of works (*Sobretexeim II*, 1972; *Carpet*, 1974) in which the distinction between 'framed' images and sculpture are blurred. Above all, his attitude to his materials became more and more daring as he grew older. After the more gestural canvases of the late 1960s he increasingly challenged the expectations of his audience with the violent imagery of works like *May 1968* (1973, page 135). This aspect has been visible since the early 1950s; *Painting*, page 116, and *Self-Portrait*, page 120, both lend support to a view of him as swinging between quiet, orderly creation and a violently physical approach. But the violent tendency in his work reached a new intensity in the series of Burnt Canvases (*Burnt Work 1*, 1973, page 137).

By any standards the Burnt Canvases are remarkably daring, but for a man in his eightieth year they represent an astonishing appetite for innovation, and reveal the continuing passion with which he approached his work. We could regard them as works in the Dadaist tradition – semi-destroyed in an act of defiance and mockery; or as having a more philosophical origin, making a point about perception and the relationship between art and the 'real world' which we are forced to see *through* these pictures; or as illustrative of the violence which he saw as at the heart of the creative act. They are not only a significant extension of his technique, but are, as the letter-paintings and the *Blue* series of the 1960s had been, perfectly in tune with their times; with the explosion of experimental and conceptual art in the 1970s, exploring the boundaries of art itself.

It seems to have been Miró's continuing interest in sculpture which fuelled his relentless technical experiments. In the latter part of his life, he certainly saw ceramics and sculpture as being at least as important as painting. And like his painting, his sculpture is almost bewilderingly varied, inexhaustibly inventive. One has only to compare two works such as *The Wind Clock*, 1967, and *Lunar Bird*, 1968 (pages 129 & 133), the one an angular, colourless, sparse tabletop piece, almost cubist in its simplicity, the other a vast white marble biomorph, exuberantly expressive. Only because we can see elements of Miró's personal language in both can we recognize them as coming from his hand.

Miró's painting also continued to defy expectation. *Triptych for the Cell of a Condemned Man* (1974, page 139) strips down his calligraphy to the merest traces. The forms are etiolated, nervous, and it is as if we are seeing his work through a kind of mist. They are beautiful but cold pictures. Miró intended them as a protest against the execution of the militant Catalan nationalist Puig Antich.[45] Despite his hermit-like existence, Miró's engagement with politics, though never formal, seems to have sharpened with old age. *May 1968* (page 135) and the *Triptych* both seem to reflect in their vehemence the political violence of the

late sixties and early seventies. Arguably, the Burnt Canvases too are a part of this process.

On the other hand, what we may call the 'public' Miró continued to produce large-scale works which invariably drew on the established painterly language which he had carried forward since the 1920s. Another ceramic mural, installed at Barcelona Airport in 1970, is quintessential, bright, playful, joky Miró, a fitting welcome to Spain's holiday coast for millions of tourists – just as later the Spanish tourist authorities were to commission from him an Espāna 'logo', still in use, a commission in which he no doubt as a Catalan took an ironic pleasure. He produced three ceramic murals for the Osaka World's Fair in the same year, but by now he and his friends were working toward the last great achievement of his career.

Barcelona was ready to honour Miró. Franco was an old, sick man and the political landscape was changing. It was decided – unofficially and with Miró's blessing – to create a foundation in his name, an Institute of Contemporary Art which would have as its centrepiece a permanent collection of his work. Commissioned in 1972, the building – designed by Josep Lluis Sert – was erected on the hill of Montjuic in a park setting. It was 'unofficially' opened on 10th June 1975, and after the death of General Franco later that year was 'officially inaugurated' in June 1976. Miró gave to it hundreds of paintings and sculptures and thousands of drawings, including his very earliest childhood works. The Galeria Maeght in Barcelona held a major retrospective of work dating from 1914 to 1974 to complement the occasion. In 1978 the Fundacio Miró received the Special Prize for Museums from the Council of Europe.

His work broadened still further; in 1977 he collaborated with a Catalan theatre group, Claca, on a production of Alfred Jarry's *Ubu Roi*, the play from which he had drawn the motif of the 'escape ladder' which occurs periodically in his art. The following year a Catalan play with his designs, *Mori el Merma*, toured Europe. His ceramics and monumental sculptures

La Fourche *1963 and* Labyrinthe Miró Céramique Ronde *1973*
The Maeght Foundation
Saint Paul de Vence

continued to be installed in prestigious sites from Germany to Japan, Spain to Wichita, culminating in several vast sculptures, including work at La Défense, Paris in 1975, *Personage and Bird* (1982) in Houston, and *Woman and Bird* (1982), his final gift to the city of Barcelona. To these projects he added tapestries, executed in collaboration with Josep Royo, in Washington, New York and Barcelona. He designed stained glass windows for the church of Saint-Frambourg in Senlis, and for the first time since 1932 he designed a ballet, *Miró l'Ucello Luce*, which premiered in Venice in 1981, his 88th year.

Miró died on Christmas Day 1983 in Palma, and was buried on Montjuic, overlooking Barcelona, near his foundation. His was not only one of the longest but one of the most varied and productive careers of any major twentieth-century artist. A late starter, not truly established until middle age, his restless and inquisitive nature and his innate optimism prevented him from standing still as an artist even at an age when most others – Dalí, Picasso, Chagall – opted for a patrician rehearsal of former glories.

Miró was a complex personality whose obsessive privacy and habitual reticence perhaps contributed to an underestimation of his talents until he was a comparatively old man. He has been in art history the victim of twin prejudices. The first error is to associate him with the convenient (and entertaining) history of the Surrealist movement, a neat historical parcel within which Miró can with little difficulty be enclosed – provided one more or less ignores the last forty years of his life. The second, much more basic and widespread prejudice is against old people, and old painters. The history of modernism, with its relentless accent upon the new, the frontier, and upon the cult of the young and of rebellion, can find no place for artists once the spotlight of 'the new' has moved on. In Miró's case this not only eliminates the vast majority of his mature works (just as with Picasso); it eliminates much of a relentless and seamless process of development, constantly renewed, ceaselessly experimental, challenging and

daring to the last. Miró's later work has usually been glossed over because the careers of most artists apparently do not conform to the pattern of his own. History will not make an exception even for the exceptional.

Despite his international reputation, everything Miro did was self-consciously Catalan, wrapped in an all-embracing mental cloak of Catalan language, thought, history, heritage and, above all, character. To be Catalan was for him to be of the earth, to be constant, to be a craftsman, to be a poet, a lover, a philosopher, a peasant, a patriot, and many other things. Perhaps most importantly, to be Catalan was to possess the twin traits which Cataluñans regard as the central pillars of their identity, and which are perfectly expressed in Miró's art. They are two sides of the Catalan coin: *seny* is reliability, order, backbone; while *rauxa* is uncontrolled passion and energy. Not only do they pervade his art, they also dictated his methods. Beyond this complex and strong self-image, Miró's Catalan identity was the basis of his extreme openness to outside stimuli, whether artistic or geographical, reflecting the openness of Cataluñan culture at the turn of the century

His sense of place was acute, and not just the *enyoranca* for the Montroig of *The Farm* or *The Hunter*. He often spoke of the energy he drew from the earth, an energy amplified when, in Montroig, or Mallorca, or Normandy, he felt his surroundings to have a metaphysical significance. Essentially it was this supernatural sense of the meanings of places, and the intense scrutiny of the minutiae of their components, human, animal, inanimate, sensory, extra-sensory, which drove him. His art is an attempt to recreate the intense experience of the moment. Even in apparently 'abstract' works, in the emaciated forms of the *Triptych for the Cell of a Condemned Man*, for example, Miró is never dealing with the abstract, always with the real world. His continual reworking of symbols demonstrates an almost alchemistic obsession with the essence of his – and our – relationship to the physical world. All his work stems from objective study, but what he was

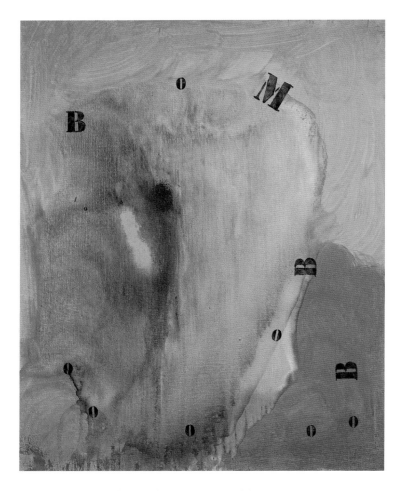

Letter and Numbers Attracted by a Spark *1968*
Oil on canvas. 116 x 114 cm
Fundacio Miró, Barcelona

landscape as the trees, as real as the rocks; he saw himself and his work as part of a great cosmic music. This is why his trees have ears, why limbs become stones, why the flight of birds above the horizon is reproduced as well as the birds themselves. 'My work is intended as a poem translated into music by a painter', he remarked[46] – a summing-up which concisely restates his realization that mere easel-painting was in the end 'rather petty'.

Easel-painting, yes, but not art; the last four decades of his life were spent as if trying to make up for this earlier limitation, making use of every available means in the search for a physical synthesis which would reproduce – or at least symbolize – the synthesis he saw between form and spirit. In this he came close to the tradition of Zen Buddhist painting. The difference is that Zen artists regard their quest as being away from human 'failings', away from passion, and away from the material, which they see as illusory. Miró shared their view of visible reality as illusion but his impulse was not toward 'nothingness' but toward (to coin a word) everythingness. His refusal to discriminate in his art between body and spirit, sound and colour, form and content, thought and word and object, in other words his insistence on the value of all things constitutes his 'surrealism', but although it crystallized in Paris it began at Montroig, in his search for the 'calligraphy' of the world. It is not French, this surrealism, but Catalan.

searching for was an understanding of the effect of the physical world upon the soul, and an expression of that effect through a grand synthesis not just of poetic symbols, but calligraphic signs, of language, of forms, of techniques, media, disciplines. And it is this all-embracing quest which is the uniquely Catalan element in his work. He recognizes similar processes at work elsewhere and acknowledges them. But these are allied to a view of the spirit as existing separately from physical reality, of being bound by it, even though these artists too are searching for the transcendent. Miró, the Catalan, saw the spirit as being *the same as* physical reality; he was part of his surroundings, his homeland, his Cataluña. His soul was as much a part of the

'Perhaps the most "Surrealist" of us all', remarked Breton, but Miró said of Breton that 'he wanted what he saw to prove what he had written'[47]. Miró, for whom the object always came first, could hardly have been more damning than that; the implication is that Breton failed to understand Miró's work, and was not really interested in it except insofar as it 'aided the cause' (a process which can be observed in Breton's relationships with painters time and again[48]). In the end, calling Miró 'a Surrealist' is the equivalent of calling Picasso 'a Cubist' or Shakespeare 'an actor'; correct, but hardly adequate.

There are two rewarding aspects to Miró's art: Miró the craftsman and Miró the poet. Rosamond Bernier relates that Henri Matisse was once asked 'whom he considered a true painter among contemporary artists: [he replied] "Miró, yes, Miró...because it doesn't matter what he represents on his canvas, but if in a certain place he put a red spot, you can be sure that it had to be there and not anywhere else. Take it away and the painting collapses"[49]. The craftsman Artigas, who knew Miró's work better than anyone, said 'Miró is a Catalan; his conception of the human is thoroughly unsentimental'; yet he summarized it not in terms of technique or of skill, as Matisse had done, but in terms of purpose: 'Above everything else he wants mankind to grasp more profoundly what being human means.'[50]

1 See, for instance, Robert Hughes, *Barcelona*, pp 22-23
2 Miró, quoted in Bernier, p 223
3 Catalan, held by the Falange to be a dialect of Spanish, is now regarded as a separate Romance language with Celtic influences.
4 Quoted in Bernier, p 223
5 JM in a letter to Jacques Dupin, in Rowell, pp 44-45
6 Mink, p10
7 See Richardson, chapter 4
8 Malet, for instance, p 8
9 See Robert Hughes, *Barcelona*, for an entertaining and pithy account of Catalan history .
10 Erben, p 42
11 Mink, p 10
12 Bernier, p 226
13 Miró is quoted by Janis Mink, p 10
14 Dupin
15 According to Miró himself, quoted in Bernier, p 228
16 Malet, p 8
17 Albert Gleizes (1881-1953) and Jean Metzinger (1883-1956) who co-wrote the theoretical treatise *Du Cubisme* in 1912, are now regarded as having had only a superficial understanding of the original intentions of Picasso, Braque and Grís. In retrospect their paintings seem to be traditional scenes given a gloss of 'cubistic' formal simplification rather than analyses of form itself. Between about 1910 and 1925, however, they were regarded as very major figures in modern art.
18 Quoted in Bucci, p 16
19 Malet, p 9
20 Quoted in Malet, p 9
21 Quoted in Bernier, p 228
22 Bernier says that 'Miró's Barcelona dealer' (Dalmau?) gave it to Picasso during a visit to Barcelona, but this seems to be an attempt to illustrate Picasso's meanness. In the unlikely event that this 'dealer' would want to give away *anything*, particularly to a man as wealthy as Picasso, he would have had no authority to do so. It seems much more likely that Miró gave him the picture, since he had brought it, and no others, from Spain, and since neither Dalmau nor anyone else was Miró's dealer in Barcelona for the next ten years or more. Picasso also acquired Miró's *Spanish Dancer* some time later, apparently in part-payment of a debt. Both are now in the Musée Picasso.
23 Quoted in Mink, p 27
24 Mink, pp 27-8
25 Hughes, p 23
26 Quoted in Mink, p 31
27 Hughes, p 27
28 Alexandrian, p 66
29 The painting may also contain a direct reference to Catalan Romanesque painting, in that the white leaf-like object on the tree with the eye is itself scattered with eyes. These are a visual pun on the snail in the foreground, but may also refer to a fresco in the Museum of Catalan Art (see Hughes, p 91) which depicts a seraph or angel with (leaf-shaped) wings covered in eyes – the *mirada fuerte* again. There also seems to be a black angel-like figure above the bull in *The Tilled Field*.
30 Alexandrian, p 73
31 Quoted in Alexandrian, p 48
32 Malet, p 12x
33 Raillard, *Miró: Les Chefs d'Œuvre*, p 80
34 Malet, p 13
35 Quoted in Bernier, p 238
36 Quoted in Erben, p 80
37 Quoted in Erben, p 83
38 Quoted in Erben, p 80
39 Quoted in Bernier, p 248
40 The article was published in *Cahiers d'Art*
41 Quoted in Bernier, p 253
42 Op cit., quoted in Malet, p 21
43 Erben, p 28
44 Bernier p 255
45 Raillard, p 140x
46 Quoted in Erben, p 227
47 Quoted in Bernier, p 234
48 Breton patronizingly pronounced Frida Kahlo a 'surrealist' on meeting her, for example, displaying a monumental lack of sensitivity to her work.
49 Bernier, p 262
50 Quoted in Erben, p 133

1893 ❧ 1983

THE PLATES

Georges Raillard, in an apt phrase, describes Montroig as Miró's 'chosen place of origin'*. Bought by his parents some six years before this painting was produced, the farmhouse at Montroig had already become Miró's spiritual home, the place to which he would, until moving to Mallorca in the 1950s, always retreat in search of calm, inspiration and renewed energy. Like many urban people, Miró's family felt the need to reassert their ties with the countryside, but since they were only a single generation away from their peasant origins the connexion was exceptionally strong. For Miró, Montroig encapsulated Cataluña.

Two strong influences are visible here; firstly, the example of his teacher Urgell, whose 'empty' landscapes, in the tradition of the Barbizon painters and of Böcklin, clearly had a lasting effect on Miró's style and, secondly, the Post-Impressionist style known as Pointillism or Divisionism, typified by Seurat and Signac. The Pointillists aimed at reproducing 'natural' light effects by dividing the palette scientifically into colour-components. Colour theory, mystical as well as scientific, always fascinated Miró.

It is tempting to identify, in the procession of crescent shapes marking the surf, the first signs of Miró's search for the 'calligraphy of things', though at this stage that concern can have been no more than incipient. The picture's concentration on 'atmosphere', on a sense of the moment rather than on the details of the scene itself, was something which he would carry forward into his mature art, though not in this manner.

Paradoxically, it was to be after a long series of pictures in which objects are minutely described that this 'metaphysical' concern would reappear.

* Raillard, *Miró: Les Chefs d'Œuvre*, p 46

The Beach at Montroig, 1916

37.3 x 45.6 cm
Fundacio Miró,
Barcelona

During the First World War Miró and other young artists congregated at Josep Dalmau's gallery in Barcelona to keep in touch with developments in the wider world. The gallery received magazines and journals from all over Europe, one of which was Pierre Reverdy's *Nord-Sud*, which carried essays and reviews, theoretical articles and poems. The arrival in Barcelona of Francis Picabia, the Dadaist painter, meant that for the first time the young Catalan artists could discuss these latest trends with someone who had had wide experience of the international avant-garde.

The first issue of *Nord-Sud* carried a detailed discussion of the principles of Cubism, but it is obviously Fauvism rather than Cubism which held Miró's interest at the time. Only in its composition does the painting show an awareness of Cubist art; a composition which is given, however, a dynamism by the vibrant stripes of colour between the objects which is at odds with their static rendition. At the centre the black and white letters are the only flat part of the canvas, which as the chief focus of the picture is again unsettling. The objects remain separate, the picture oddly diffuse despite the 'elective affinities' between them which Miró perhaps intended to point to by including a volume of Goethe. On the other hand, the presence of this Northern work in a Southern painting may have been the intended pun. Another possibility is that the book is a reference to Goethe's interest in colour theory.

Nord-Sud, 1917

62 x 70 cm
Adrien Maeght,
Paris

In contrast to the *Nord-Sud*, this is a strongly unified composition, in which fauvist colour has been joined to another influence, that of Vincent Van Gogh. The picture is constructed using the strong black outlines and rippling forms typical of the Dutchman, but Miró chooses to break up the surface into separate facets, within which the brushstrokes of colour are not rendered parallel to the outlines, as they would be in Van Gogh's later work.

Whereas *The Beach at Montroig* (page 45) was a poetic, suggestive landscape, this is a straightforward portrayal of the play of light on landscape forms, and is very different from the tradition of Urgell, Miró's teacher. Although Van Gogh is the most obvious influence, the way the landscape is built up suggests an awareness of the work of Paul Cézanne, while the palette derives from Matisse. Miró has combined these influences very successfully, and there is little sign here of the fascination with using surface patterning to disrupt the viewer's sense of perspective which was shortly to become a strong feature of his work.

This is one of a series of landscapes painted in 1917-18 in which Miró experimented with very high colour in what were essentially traditional landscape formats. His sense of colour had always been strong, and these pictures demonstrate that his later work was also built on a sound grasp of traditional composition.

The Church at Ciurana, 1917

46 x 55 cm
Private collection

_____

In contrast to the deep perspective of *The Church at Ciurana* (page 49), here it is the surface patterning and shallow picture space which are immediately striking. Miró has chosen to show his close friend and fellow-student wearing striped pyjamas to exaggerate this effect. The inclusion of the Japanese print is an acknowledgment of the source of this tendency, so important to nineteenth-century artists such as Toulouse-Lautrec and Van Gogh. It is to the latter that the overall composition of the picture (and the use of a plain bright yellow background) is indebted, but the modelling of the figure once again utilizes Matisse's systems of colour. The Fauves were also, of course, influenced by Japanese art in their pictorial organization.

Miró's interest in oriental art affected his work very strongly at times, notably in the late 1950s and early 1960s. The Japanese tradition of using expressive lines to suggest form undoubtedly influenced his own mature work and his search for a 'calligraphy of things'. Despite its precision, Japanese art – and in particular Japanese landscape painting – is basically a suggestive rather than a descriptive exercise. While we have seen in *The Beach at Montroig* that Miró was attracted to this kind of art, it was only after the highly detailed works of the early 1920s that this impulse was to reassert itself in his work.

The inclusion of the painter's or the sitter's palette, 'hung' on a wall which may not be there, is yet another disruption of the picture's space. If the palette is an emblem rather than a 'real' object, is the print itself really 'behind' the sitter?

Portrait of E. C. Ricart, 1917

81 x 65 cm
Metropolitan Museum of Art,
New York

As in *The Church at Ciurana* and the *Portrait of E. C. Ricart*, Miró is again attempting to combine 'opposing' styles in a single canvas. Here the background of richly patterned hanging and carpet is derived from Matisse, and has the effect of compressing the picture-space. Our perception of this complex surface is, however, undermined by the very full modelling of the nude. The body is divided into schematic masses, which add to the superficial patterning, but these masses are themselves deeply shaded, so that the figures seem to both retreat into the patterning and stand out from it.

Although the nude is rendered in a 'cubistic' manner, it is not strictly Cubist; there is no real disruption of perspective. Miró had probably read the influential theoretical treatise *Du Cubisme* by the French painters Albert Gleizes and Jean Metzinger, whose art borrowed Cubist mannerisms without attempting the dissection of forms pioneered by Picasso, Gris and Braque. The modelling of the face strongly recalls the *Portrait of E. C. Ricart*, but the colouring of the figure is essentially Cubist rather than Fauvist.

Interestingly, we can see for the first time a formal element which was to be carried forward into his mature vocabulary. The right breast, shown in profile, is later simplified into a frequently repeated characteristic of his female forms. One can find it, for instance, in the first of the *Constellations* series (page 111), and in *A Drop of Dew…Awakens Rosalie* (page 109).

A further stylistic anomaly is the inclusion on the right of another 'Cubist' passage in which parallel forms suggested in grey and brown clash with the flat backcloth. Since they echo the edge of the hanging they appear to be standing further forward than the cloth itself. These in turn are playfully juxtaposed with the leaves of the plant, which (as in *Nord-Sud*) do not prevent us from seeing the far side of the rim of the pot. The plant thus bridges the two conflicting spaces.

Standing Female Nude, 1918
152 x 122 cm
The Saint Louis Art Museum

This important picture, a view of the farm at Montroig, marks the beginning of what Miró termed his 'detailist' phase, which culminated in *The Farm* (page 59) and which led directly to his development of a personal language of signs. It was in the context of this picture that he first mentioned to E. C. Ricart his concern with the 'calligraphy of things'; his conviction that by minute rendition of selected formal characteristics of an object one could communicate its reality more precisely than by traditional means. Thus he need not show every leaf of a tree, or every branch, but could instead show the typical or essential patterns they create. Similarly, there was no need to render every blade of the grass which the donkey is eating, just enough to show that that is what it is doing. The logical extension (or reduction) of this idea in later works is the portrayal of a single leaf on a single branch to signify a tree, and then a transformation into a biomorphic form which recalls the leaf and the branch without truly resembling them.

There is still a strong flavour of Cubism in this picture, despite its fairly conventional perspective. The use of colour, too, is much more restrained than in earlier works, though not reduced to the muted greys and ochres which typify mainstream Cubism. It was probably that school, however, rather than Dadaist art which gave Miró the idea of showing the surrounding landscape 'in the sky'. The box- or room-like perspective suggests a prism which refracts the surroundings into this unfamiliar configuration. Miró, by this original device, was trying to encompass in the canvas the totality of his experience of the place, his awareness not only of what he could see but of Montroig's place in the landscape of Cataluña. As the influence of Cubism faded, Miró was to pursue this aim single-mindedly through a progression of formal experiments.

The Kitchen Garden with Donkey, 1918

60 x 70 cm
Moderna Museet,
Stockholm

The last picture which Miró finished before travelling to Paris (he took the unfinished *The Farm* with him) was this rather enigmatic portrait. The subject may well have been imaginary; what is clear is that the style of the *Portrait of E. C. Ricart* (page 51) has been left far behind. Perhaps the closest resemblance is to the work of Amedeo Modigliani, recalled by the formal symmetry of the features and the sinuous line, the columnar neck and the shallow modelling as well as the plain, loosely worked background. But although it is possible that Miró could have seen one of Modigliani's works reproduced, there is no evidence that he had. On the other hand, while the reduction of the outline and delicate brushwork parallel these tendencies in his landscape painting, it is difficult to make a case that this picture was motivated by the same fierce concentration on the 'calligraphy of things'. Only in the sparse, evenly spaced eyelashes can we discern something which might hint at his concerns in *The Kitchen Garden with Donkey*.

This was the last canvas Miró produced which had any direct relationship to established canons of painting until 1937. The move to Paris was to confirm that his future lay in radical innovation rather than in the renewal of traditional genres.

Portrait of a Young Girl, 1919

33 x 28 cm
Fundacio Miró,
Barcelona

Miró said that he worked on this canvas for eight hours a day over a period of eight months. In it he attempts to represent his 'chosen place of origin', the farmhouse at Montroig, as the very essence of Cataluña. By extension, it is as much a painting about himself as it is a landscape.

The detailism first attempted in *The Kitchen Garden with Donkey* (page 55) is here taken to an extreme. It is noticeable that Miró has abandoned the Cubist mannerisms of the earlier work, both in the perspective and in the portrayal of objects. But the objects are not shown naturalistically. Instead they have a granular, inky texture, very like items in a catalogue. Possibly he meant them to resemble woodcuts, and thus give the painting a flavour of folk art, a tendency which becomes very clear in slightly later canvases.

Miró's presence at Montroig, and his absence from it, are signified by the inclusion of the Parisian newspaper *L'Intransigéant* in the foreground. But it is not really a painting about loss, except perhaps in the sense of a temporary homesickness. Miró could, and frequently did, return to Montroig. Robert Hughes describes it as a painting of *enyorança*, a longing for a lost past, but this too is only half the story. Miró speaks at this time of a 'new Catalan art', and the picture contains few traces of what he regarded as a corrupt and devalued French tradition. This astonishingly vivid and dream-like picture contains little which suggests the past, in fact. It is full of modern, mass-produced objects; its people are working, its animals and plants thriving. It does not mourn, it celebrates. It represents a better present, not a better past.

The Farm contains several objects and motifs which recur throughout Miró's later output: the snail, goat, birds, moon, dog and so on. There are also signs of the process of reduction of objects into clusters of single components which was to typify his work. The tree, for example, while still possessing multiple branches and leaves (though not as many as 'in reality'), has on its trunk a few giant thorns to signify its prickliness.

The painting was considered unsaleable: neither Cubist nor realist, not obviously part of any recognized movement or tendency, and presenting a scene in which objects were placed seemingly with childish lack of grace, no-one in Paris could understand it and no-one found it attractive. Miró's friends advised him to cut it up and sell the pieces separately.

The Farm, 1921-22

132 x 147 cm
National Gallery of Art,
Washington

The French title which Miró gave to this picture, *Terre Labourée*, might be better translated as 'Worked Earth', since although a ploughed (not tilled) field is visible, the subject is once again the whole farm of Montroig and the countryside of Cataluña in general.

Miró had taken 'detailism' to its logical conclusion in *The Farm*, and in this transitional canvas is searching for a new way to express the meaning of the place. We have seen in the *The Kitchen Garden with Donkey* that he was prepared to use experimental techniques to 'get more into' the picture than traditional perspective would permit. This method was abandoned in *The Farm*, where he hoped that his fierce concentration on objects would produce this same effect – that the picture would express much more than the sum of its parts. Now again he is attempting to say more about Montroig than the literal transcription of its contents would allow. And here it is true to say that his method for the first time is Surrealist rather than realist.

The painting stands as one of the very first 'pure' Surrealist works. Many other artists – Ernst, Masson and Arp, for example – were still producing works which were strongly flavoured by their Dadaist backgrounds. Miró, however, has arrived at Surrealism from an altogether different direction. Just as in *The Kitchen Garden with Donkey* he shows only a small area of grass to indicate what the donkey is doing, and in *The Farm* this process was taken further by the large thorns on the tree-trunk, here he takes another step by giving objects new forms based on these simplified elements, rather than attaching the simplified forms to essentially realistic objects. The prickly pear has just one serrated edge on each gigantic 'leaf'; the carob tree's canopy is reduced to an oval to which thorns are attached in a fringe. But not everything in the picture is to be interpreted in this manner. The horse and dog, for example, retain more of their usual appearance, though again with many simplified and exaggerated characteristics.

The other new element of the picture is that Miró gives some objects appendages – ear, eye, flags – which

The Tilled Field, 1923

66 x 94 cm
The Solomon R. Guggenheim Museum,
New York

represent nothing physical at all, but function metaphysically. This is a painting about the passage of time and the immemoriality of Montroig – the ploughman uses a 'prehistoric' ox – and the tree is thus shown as a 'being' which has heard and seen everything around it through the ages, and continues to do so. Similarly, the exaggerated size of the horse's legs and hooves signifies its bond with the earth, from which it draws its energy.

If *The Farm* can be regarded as the last product of Miró's formative years, and *The Tilled Field* the picture in which he begins to work out a new direction, then *Catalan Landscape* stands as the first complete expression of his mature aesthetic. Essentially this is the style in which he would work for the next fifty years.

The process of reduction of forms into single components and/or into calligraphic signs has here reached a stage where few objects are immediately interpretable. Indeed, some resist interpretation completely, or at least remain ambivalent. The figure of the Hunter himself, a stick-man to whom are attached cap, eye, ear, moustache, beard, heart and the almond-like sprouting form which Miró used to signify the anus or sexual organs, carries a gun (reduced to a long black triangle) and a smaller triangle which might be a pouch hanging from his arm. We could suppose, therefore, that Miró has decided to represent inanimate objects as geometric forms. But this does not help us with the conical shapes on the sea and the shore (perhaps a boat, and on the shore therefore an upturned, beached boat). We should note too that the rabbit in the foreground has a geometric 'foot' from which four claws protrude. And how are we to understand the 'set square' in the lower left-hand corner (a device, like the cones, which became a frequent sight in his work)?

On the other hand, we can be reasonably certain that the single leaf on the single branch attached to the pale circular form represents the same tree which occupied that position in *The Farm* and *The Tilled Field*. The white form might indicate the whitewashed lower trunk visible in the first of those two pictures, and the eye seems to confirm it in a reference to the second. The two black circles are presumably rabbit-holes, and the device with a ladder, wheels and flags in the upper left-hand corner is the horse-powered mill visible in the background of *The Farm*.

A striking difference to earlier works is the overt reference to sex. Here the sun is represented by a sign which, as we can see from later works, is an anal/vaginal symbol. The Hunter's genitals have also been shown,

Catalan Landscape (The Hunter), 1923-24

65 x 100 cm
Museum of Modern Art,
New York

as have the rabbit's (the egg-like form near the triangle). There is a turd on the left of the picture, and the butterfly near the rabbit's head is defecating. The 'tree'-form itself is breast-like. So Miró is here identifying the Catalan landscape, and Catalan life, with (his) sexuality, and linking this with other basic natural forces: blood, excrement, the life-giving power of the sun.

On the right, the letters 'sard' are a reference to the sardine, a staple of the Catalan diet and a local sexual/fertility symbol. In a preliminary sketch, the whole word is visible.

This little collage (the moon is glued on) is an early example of Miró's 'poem-painting' style. By this time closely involved with the nucleus of Surrealist artists, and already deeply interested in poetry, Miró was searching for a form which would bridge the gap between these two means of expression.

The picture makes playful use of formal parallels – the letter A, the moustache, the figure's raised arms – in a space which is devoid of references to landscape except that the sky is at the top and a flower grows at the bottom. Between these is an area in which the disruptive and comic effects of the gust of wind have been shown by a scattering of forms which create a new dialogue as they refer to each other. This is the kind of 'network' of correspondences which Miró was later to develop so richly in the *Constellations* series (page 111).

The wind is celebrated as a force which upsets expectations, subverts (bourgeois) dignity and produces intriguing 'accidental' associations between objects. It is as much a symbol of the new cultural force of Surrealism as a humorous little anecdote.

The Wind, 1924

60 x 46.4 cm
Acquavella Galleries,
New York

Here the body of a woman is represented as a vase in which 'flowers' representing her charms are placed. Each stem ends in a part of her body or a symbol – eye, teeth, vagina, comet. One ends in her profile. From the vase protrude her arms and legs (one of which is hairy, one shaved).

Although we can find much in the picture to relate to earlier and to later works, it ought also to be looked at in the context of the broader concerns of the Surrealists with women and sexuality. From the beginning, Woman was identified by Breton, the chief theoretician of the movement, as 'the most marvellous problem', and celebrated as the repository of all that was mysterious. On the one hand, women were unintelligible, irrational beings, subject to powerful natural forces, and were the objects of an attention which at times did not differ much from the scrutiny of doctors and psychologists. But at the same time, they were to be venerated as sphinx-like creatures who had access to arcane knowledge. Both these tendencies were shot through with a fascination with female sexuality and desire, the product of a male regime which found these ideas both exciting and threatening. Woman was therefore always represented throughout the Surrealist canon as something other, different, abnormal, whether as goddess, whore, patient or seeress.

Miró's blonde is dissected, reduced to component objects of desire, and equated with a decorative vase of flowers. Her massive feet indicate her connexion to Mother Earth, and the energy she draws from it.

My Blonde's Smile, 1924
88 x 115 cm
Private collection

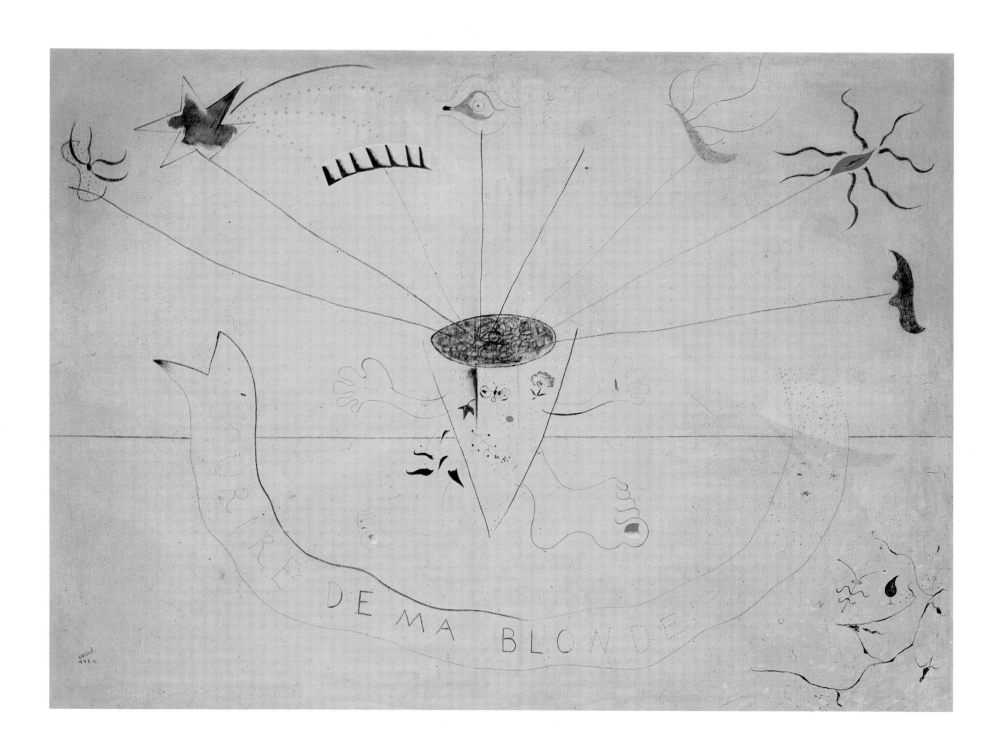

This is almost a traditional still-life, in that it symbolizes the connexion between the fruits of the earth and the natural forces which produced them. The bottle's base has become a volcano, and the label a play on the words *vi* (Catalan = 'wine') and its root in Latin *vita*, 'life' and thus a multiplicity of other puns, including perhaps *vit* (French slang = 'penis').

The resemblance between the whiskered snake-like creature and the rabbit in *Catalan Landscape* is striking; in both cases it is the eye which holds our attention and the angle of its movement into the canvas is similar. Indeed, the clawed creature in the foreground of *The Tilled Field* is another ancestor, and even perhaps the tiny lizard in *The Farm*, which confronts the snail in the same way. The insect too has become a permanent addition to this menagerie, here radiating beams of energy from its eyes. Other signs are also paralleled elsewhere; the white vine-stem to the left of the wine bottle can be found on the vase-body in *My Blonde's Smile* (page 67) and the river in the upper right-hand corner echoes the sky-landscape of *The Kitchen Garden with Donkey*.

Above his signature Miró has written 'Ars meus franco' ('My French art'), perhaps an ironic comment on the Cubist tradition of still-life painting.

The Wine Bottle, 1924

73 x 65 cm
Fundacio Miró,
Barcelona

According to his article 'I dream of a large studio', Miró's drawings for this painting were the results of hallucinations brought on by hunger. While the composition presents a new complexity, and pushes even further his distortions of form, I believe his inspiration must have been to combine the intention to 'catalogue' his surroundings, as in *The Farm*, with the pictorial language he bad developed since. In other words, this is a catalogue of his internal landscape rather than that of Cataluña. The setting is his studio, and it is as if his previous works have come to life at the Carnival. Miró himself – or rather the Hunter, the archetypal Catalan, with his moustache, beard, pipe and hat – is represented as Harlequin. In the lower left corner is the cockerel which flies over Montroig in *The Tilled Field*, and on the right is the farmhouse kitchen table and fish from a work of 1920, *Still Life with Rabbit*. Outside, the moon corresponds to the sun in *Catalan Landscape*; the insect reappears on the tip of the moustache and emerging from a die; the eyes, ear, cones, set square, flags and ladder are all familiar.

The mildew and cracks on the wall around the window refer back to the ancient walls of *The Farm*, but they also record how Miró, following the advice of Leonardo da Vinci, found inspiration in the patterning of the decaying walls and ceiling of his studio: he would lie in bed and sketch the ideas which flowed from this exercise. Miró greatly admired Leonardo: 'the most intelligent of them all, genius personified! What are we compared to him?'* Leonardo's advice was hailed by the Surrealists as proof that they were on the right track, and the method would have appealed to Miró, who drew so much from his intense concentration of the details of his surroundings, transforming them through the power of his gaze.

* Quoted in Erben, p 80

The Carnival of Harlequin, 1924-25

66 x 93 cm
Allbright Knox Art Gallery,
Buffalo

During 1924 and 1925 Miró made a series of drawings and paintings on carefully squared-up surfaces. He seems to have been attempting to give his new repertoire of signs a kind of absolute exactitude; there is nothing free about their construction. It should be borne in mind that whereas many of his canvases suggest someone working out forms 'automatically', composing them on canvas, this was never the case until he began to experiment with direct painting during the 1950s. Until then, with the possibe exception of *Oh! Un de ces messieurs* all his works were the result of (often very many) careful and exact studies and sketches.

Here the figure of the archetypal Catalan, the hunter once again, is reduced to two lines, body and arms, a sphere for a head, a red cap and a moustache which implies, by its position, a phallic connotation. In the right-angled 'hand', or perhaps the crook of the arm, he holds an area of thick white paint, pierced with small holes. Raillard identifies this as the land itself,* though there are no formal parallels for this elsewhere in Miró's work. Given the associations of the figure, however, this would make sense.

*Raillard, p 74

The Catalan, 1925
100 x 81 cm
Musée National d'Art Moderne,
Paris

Even by Miró's standards, this is an enigmatic canvas. Who are these 'gentlemen' and what have they made or done?

The forms are just recognizable as things we have seen before: the sky and stars in *The Wine Bottle*, and perhaps the snake (here with a red, forked tongue) from the same picture. This, however, does look like a spontaneous picture, painted perhaps in anger (is the writing a record of a disparaging comment on Miró and the Surrealists?).

This is perhaps the closest thing Miró produced to a Dadaist image; an anti-picture, an insult to the expectations of the 'art lover'.

Oh! Un de ces messieurs
qui a fait tout ça!
(Oh! One of those Gentlemen
who has made all that), 1925

130 x 95 cm
Private collection

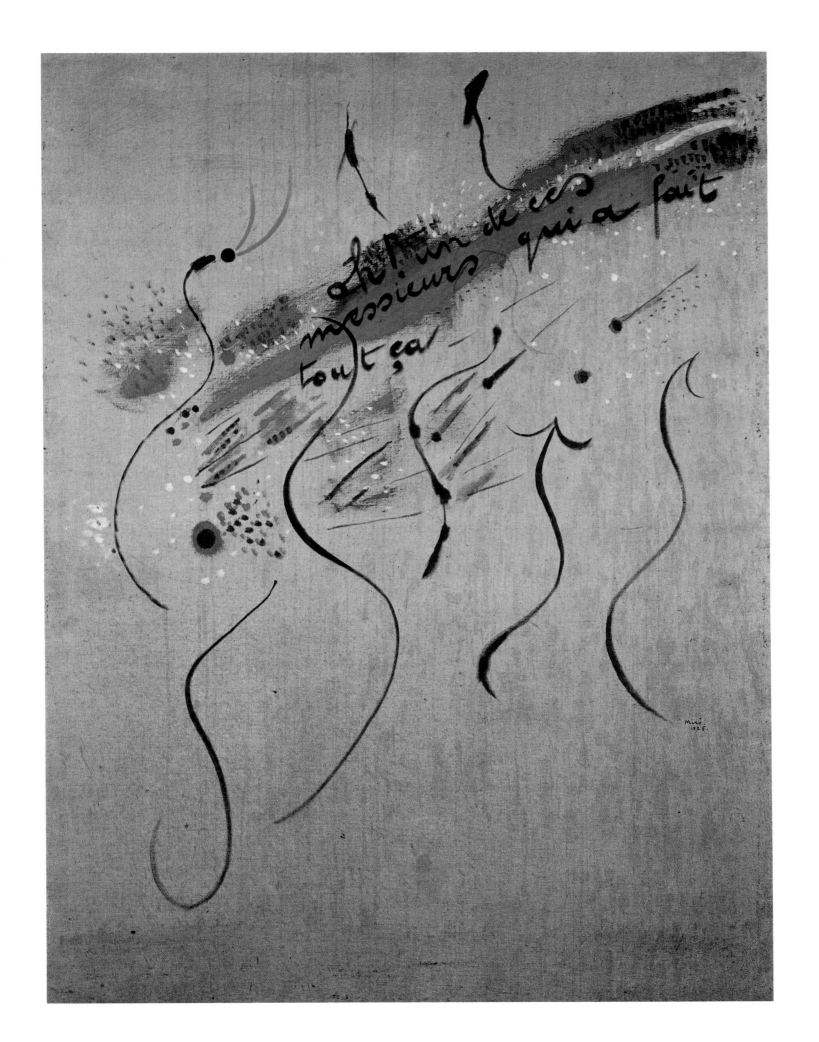

Drawings for this work show that it was worked out precisely before it was painted. The format is that of the seaside landscape familiar from *Catalan Landscape* (page 63), but within this little is self-evident. The human form lying partly within the dotted circle is obviously the sleeper, and the circle may indicate the enclosed world of the realm of sleep. The white form has been interpreted as a combination of a house and a sleeping woman* but I would suggest that it is in fact a clock which is 'melting' in a visual parallel of the temporal disruption of dreams. The arms of the clock point to the number and connect with the horizon, a visual metaphor for the boundary between the real and unseen worlds. In the sky the sun is once again transformed into a sexual symbol by its covering of hair-like cloud, the cloud of unconsciousness which hides it from the sleeper. Above the sea the wing-like form seems to be based on the forms of birds and waves present in *Catalan Landscape*, and suggests the flight of the sleeper into the world of dreams.

The effect of the painting is one of stillness and expectation, the 'pregnant moment' we see in de Chirico's dream-like urban landscapes and, I would venture, in Miró's early work, *The Beach at Montroig* (page 45).

* Raillard, p 78

The Siesta, 1925

113 x 146 cm
Musée National d'Art Moderne,
Paris

The connexion in Miró's mind between the dream-world and the blue heavens suggested in *The Siesta* (page 77) is confirmed here. This connexion between earth and sky is central to Miró's work, and the things which connect them – birds, insects, the ladder – constantly recur, symbols of freedom and escape from the world of the ordinary into that of heightened, truer perception. Once again the picture's simplicity and the apparent casualness of the blue form are belied by preparatory sketches in which this form is exactly placed and defined.

Miró is challenging us to accept the absolute reality of the dream. In effect he is saying that his painting of dream has the veracity, the conclusive objectivity, of a photograph. It is thus at one and the same time entirely serious, an expression of the central tenet of Surrealism, and deliberately playful and subversive, since to label it a 'photo' is to take an outrageous liberty with our beliefs and preconceptions.

This was a work of which Miró remained very fond and very proud. It belonged to his friend Max Ernst, with whom he collaborated on the ballet *Romeo and Juliet* in 1926. Many years later Miró was in America, at a party given in his honour by the Abstract Expressionist painter Robert Rauschenberg. Rauschenberg suddenly picked up a pot of blue paint and 'slung it at the glass skylight, turning it blue by way of tribute to Miró's *This is the colour of my dreams*'.* It is one of the icons not only of Surrealism but of the whole of modern painting.

* Bernier, p 236

This Is the Colour of My Dreams, 1925

86.5 x 129.5 cm
Collection of M. and Mme Pierre Matisse,
New York

Photo

*ceci est la couleur
de mes rêves.*

This work is one of a series of dream-paintings executed in 1926-27. Miró once again reproduced the elements of the picture from an exact preparatory drawing. Here he seems to be interested in the chromatic relationships of colours and the effect of the thinly stained background on our perception of space. What appears from one angle to be a flat surface becomes from another (for example, seen from slightly to one side) an almost three-dimensional image, with the forms 'floating' in front of the backdrop. In addition he uses the angular lines connecting areas of colour to deepen the picture space.

Miró said that none of his works was abstract, that 'everything proceeds from the object'. While elements within this canvas bear a resemblance to established symbols (comet-like forms, stars, hairs), it is not a picture open to interpretation in the same way as, for example, *The Siesta* (page 77). What we can see is literally unearthly, objects and forms which bear no relation to 'real' ones, and which obey only their own laws and logic. Yet his implication is that even here he began with the physical world, transforming it gradually until he arrived at a completely new poetic reality.

Painting, 1926

100 x 81 cm
Private collection

Three preparatory drawings for this work reveal the process described in the previous caption perfectly. Originally a drawing of two swans on water, this was refined until one bird assumed the quasi-geometric form on the left and the other the still swan-like white form on the right, with the water becoming the black and yellow wave below. The resulting painting is not supposed to show 'swans', however, but merely to exist in its own right and to refer only to itself.

By these means Miró was searching for a visual language which had the same 'naturalness', the same sense of inevitability, as the physical world. By always beginning with the object, the resultant work would retain something of its natural appearance; would become, in effect, a new thing, as if the artist had invented the tree or the swan. Undoubtedly Miró was indebted here to some extent to his close friend Jean (Hans) Arp, his neighbour in the rue Blomet. Arp had been associated with the Dada movement in Switzerland during the First World War, but had nevertheless resolutely pursued his own programme, a one-man movement. While his Dadaist friends were producing satirical collages and elegant mechanical jokes using cut-out machinery, Arp was concentrating on creating an art which took natural forms – twigs, leaves, stones – and transformed them into new objects. That is precisely what Miró is doing here ten years later. Arp's art continued to have a powerful effect on Miró, in particular on the development of his sculpture, *Construction* (1930, page 93) for example.

Painting, 1927
19 x 24.3 cm
Private collection

One of a series of large-format landscapes created at Montroig in the summer of 1927, *Landscape with Cockerel* restates the scene of *The Farm* and *The Tilled Field* as a place of connexion between dream and reality. The 'escape ladder' descends from the sky to the feet of the viewer, or the painter, who can thus move effortlessly between the two. Once again the cockerel crows in its flight over the farmhouse; once again the mill is on the horizon in the place where we saw it in *The Farm* and in *Catalan Landscape* (page 63). The almond-like shapes (which have a sexual significance) here seem to float over the land, casting no shadows though they are themselves shaded. They may be fruits, eggs, boulders, seeds, or all of these things.

The emptiness of the scene is in stark contrast to earlier Montroig pictures. The implication of the ladder and of the cockerel, a kind of sentinel at this doorway between reality and dream (or perhaps, as in *The Tilled Field*, between night sleep and day waking) is that the other items so lovingly described in *The Farm* are no longer necessary to Miró's encapsulation of the place. *The Farm* was a painting about Cataluña, but this is a painting about the personal significance of Cataluña to Miró, not in terms of an inherited or assumed cultural tradition but of its spiritual potency. He no longer felt the need to celebrate his nationality overtly, only as the transforming power of his vision and the source from which he drew his strength.

Landscape with Cockerel, 1927
130 x 195 cm
Private collection

Miró brought back from a trip to the Netherlands several postcards of Old Master paintings, including Jan Steen's *The Cat's Dancing Lesson* which formed the starting point of this picture. Like the cracks in his studio wall, or one of his own studies of everyday objects, these paintings were gradually transformed in a series of detailed drawings as he redesigned their internal forms one by one. The results were a series of comical and disturbing works.

In Jan Steen's picture a group of men and women are gathered around a table. While one plays a pipe, another lifts a cat onto its hind legs, making it 'dance', while the others laugh. A bearded man looks down from a window above, and a spaniel gazes up from the foreground.

Miró has eliminated the left-hand end of the table, and welded together parts of the figures, vastly exaggerating some details and minimizing others. Almost every element in the canvas is traceable to a feature of the original, but the dynamic of the composition has been transformed by the enormous encircling 'arms' which held the cat in the original but here squeeze the dog in a typically scatological joke, like a bagpipe. The cat itself corresponds to the large white area, but is also suggested by a passage on the 'lap' of the woman in blue playing the pipe, which is not derived from the folds of the dress in Steen's picture. The arrow which crosses the dog's elongated neck refers to the collar of the original animal, and to the foot of the piper which echoes its line precisely. Miró is thus using the originals' geometry as a means of creating a new dynamic rhythm, complementing the music of the scene. There is a strong parallel in Miró's method here with the work of Salvador Dalí, whose 'paranoiac-critical' approach relied on similar transformations, and who often chose to rework Old Master paintings himself. The brown head in this picture is particularly reminiscent of the work of Miró's fellow-Catalan. But the intentions of the two painters were very different: Dalí's work is highly self-referential and, while it seeks to illustrate a surreality, it rarely if ever displays the

Dutch Interior II, 1928

92 x 73 cm
Peggy Guggenheim Collection,
Venice

poetic optimism which is the hallmark of so much that Miró produced. Dalí is not concerned with escape, or with the revolutionary transformation of the real world. He is entirely obsessed with the workings of his own mind. Painting in itself does not interest him; it is a means to an end, and his pictures are critiques, rather than positive redefinitions, of reality.

The title suggests another transformation from an Old Master portrait; in fact the starting point was a diagram of a Junkers internal combustion engine torn from a magazine. 'Junkers – The Finest German Brand' evidently decided the Queen's nationality, but her physical form is so extremely removed from her mechanical ancestry that we could never guess it. There were no less than sixteen preparatory drawings for this work, now in the Fundacio Miró, and the following note is on one of them: 'very concentrated/pure spirit/no painting!/but very rich/as rich as colour/precious material/very finely painted'.

Although the broad divisions of warm colour suggest an internal space, these notes suggest ('pure spirit') that this is not real space at all. The figure itself, head turned aside and hands on hips, is reminiscent of a flamenco dancer, but her position within this space is equivocal.

The presentation of mechanical devices and engines as female bodies was typical of the work of Francis Picabia, whom Miró had known in Barcelona, and Picabia's old partner in crime, Marcel Duchamp. Whereas these two might simply have left the machine alone except to rechristen her, Miró seems to have known exactly what kind of picture he wanted to create, and found a focus for it by accident. He spoke of this process in his work as the 'shock' of seeing an object, of suddenly recognizing a new form in a familiar thing and then working back to that original shock through his drawings.

Queen Louise of Prussia, 1929

81 x 100 cm
Meadows Museum, Southern University,
Dallas

Miró forgot the name of the painter of the original *Portrait of Mrs Mills* – it mattered little to him. It was in fact George Engleheart, a pupil of Reynolds and the leading miniaturist of eighteenth-century England. This was a fact discovered by the American art historian James Thrall Soby, although many sources still mistakenly credit the original to John Constable.

The picture has a distinct flavour of satirical humour. The proud bourgeoise has been turned into a comical, sexualized 'personage', a statuesque, Surrealist pin-up. Among the many indignities she has suffered is the loss of her arms, emphasizing her defencelessness in the face of Miró's attentions; her breast and wasp-waist have been wildly exaggerated; and her hair and jewellery redefined like wire sculpture.

The painting has an angularity new to Miró's work, a sense of tension in the lines absent from the fluid rhythms of *Dutch Interior II* (page 87) or *Queen Louise of Prussia* (page 89). He was in fact entering a phase of uncertainty and depression, and turned increasingly to collage and to sculpture for a while. When he returned to painting he was to produce altogether more sombre and then increasingly violent and anguished images.

Portrait of Mrs Mills
in 1750, 1929

116 x 89 cm
Museum of Modern Art,
New York

Strongly reminiscent of the work of Miró's friend and neighbour Jean Arp, Miró's *Construction* differs crucially in that it refers to the human figure (a woman standing beneath the red sun), and is thus a continuation by other means of his earlier work. Arp's forms are 'pure', referring only to themselves; his constructed and sculpted works never refer, as this does, to the framed picture or the traditional landscape format. Arp himself dismissed any suggestion of influence.*

Miró's piece uses roughly planed wood as a background – an indication of his increasing interest in textured surfaces, which saw him work, around the beginning of the 1930s, on such media as sandpaper, cloth and concrete. Arp's pieces rarely use unworked and unpainted wood.

Perhaps the most interesting aspect of this work is the scattering of staples which Miró has attached to the surfaces of the white and red forms. These have no parallel at all in his painted works; he rarely if ever gave any hint as to the textural qualities of the forms in his paintings. The staples may have a kinetic function; as can be seen from the photograph, shadows play an important role here. There is also a suggestion of violence in their penetrative action.

The dynamic of the piece is internal; it is an essentially static image enclosed within the framing background of planks. As Miró's interest in construction and sculpture increased, and his skill in them evolved, it was their dynamic potential which increasingly interested him. He was fascinated by the relationship of a piece to its surroundings, and the disruptive or transformatory effect of its introduction into the 'real world'.

* Raillard, p 96

Construction, 1930

91.1 x 70.2 x 16.2 cm
Museum of Modern Art,
New York

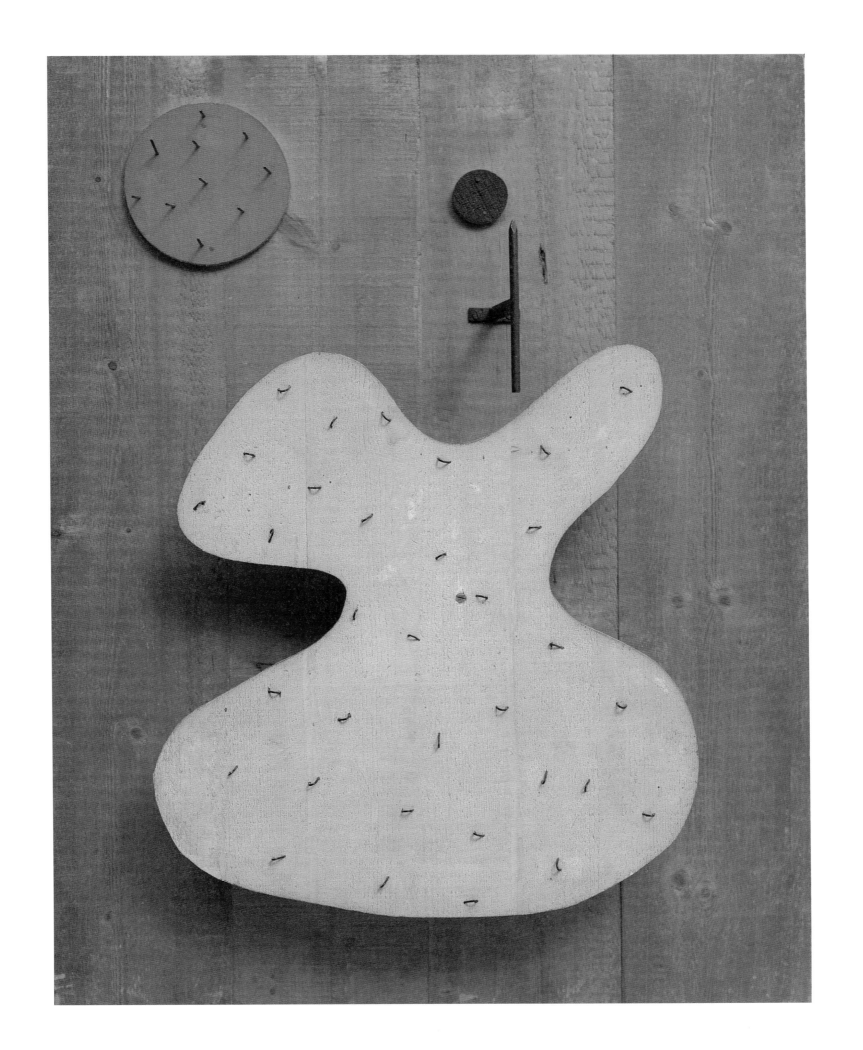

The identification of the previous work with the female body seems to be confirmed by this example from the same series, as does the implicit violence. Here the 'subject' is clearly a sexual encounter, and the guitar-shaped form is at once torso and vagina, fringed with hair. The red male figure is phallically erect, the 'head' of the white, female figure echoes this form and an 'arm' partially surrounds it, implying either desire or resistance, or both.

But what of the constructed aspect of the work? The piece of wood acts only as a background once again, but is itself placed on a mesh. Should this be read as having a symbolic value as well as a purely formal one? The net suggests space, but it also implies capture and imprisonment. The wooden plaque is itself like a cell within the wires, from which the couple cannot escape.

Miró was always very reticent about the sexual connotations of his work. Yet nowhere was sexual activity more apparent in his art than in the period roughly between 1929 and 1939, when by his own admission he was undergoing a crisis of confidence – not in his ability, but in the value of what he was doing. With the unfolding political crises of the 1930s the anxiety of his imagery increases, and very often this anxiety is expressed through a language in which female sexuality and violence are clearly linked. It may be too simplistic to say that his creative frustration found expression in or was eased by his often brutal treatment of the female body, but there can be little doubt that both his personal, creative crisis and the urgent danger to democracy were intimately connected to this theme. The creative urge and the sexual drive are closely linked, as many artists will testify; they draw on the same reserves of energy. For a man like Miró, for whom the process of creation was at once an intellectual struggle and a violent encounter with his materials, total involvement in his work must have meant that any artistic crisis would have had repercussions on other aspects of his personality.

Object-Painting, 1931

30 x 26 cm
Musée National d'Art Moderne,
Paris

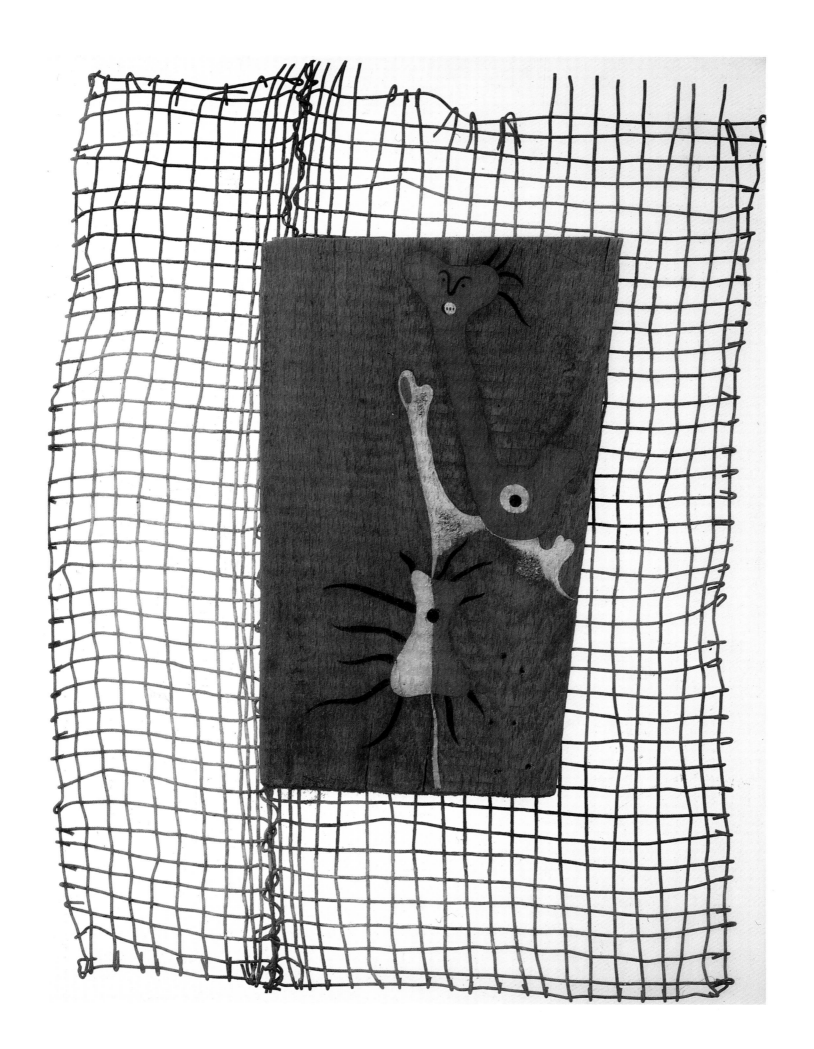

When he returned to painting Miró seems to have struggled to achieve what once had come naturally, if not easily, to him. The series of which this is an example displays a singular lack of energy, of the *joie de vivre* which we associate with so much of his output both before and later. Against backgrounds of sombre browns, greys and blues washed together like clouds of smog, flat, increasingly threatening forms float, predominantly black. While elements are recognizable – the claw/hand, the wheel – most are not. Their outlines, once taut, are now slack and indecisive. They do not communicate with each other, nor do they have the dynamic sense of movement which gives such a vivid sense of animation even to a canvas as sparse as *Landscape with Cockerel*, let alone *The Carnival of Harlequin*. Even his ability to group these forms gracefully within the frame – an ability which is at times almost musical – has here deserted him, or has been deliberately suppressed. The starting points for the paintings in this series were collages, often using pictures of objects cut from store catalogues. Here the forms on the right, for example, were originally a spoon and fork. Miró used this method, or similar processes, all his life, often taking weeks or even months to find the right arrangement of forms before beginning the long process of transforming them into a painting. But whereas in later life he enjoyed the almost monkish contemplation which this approach allowed, in the early thirties it seems that it was caution and uncertainty which necessitated it.

Painting, 1933

97 x 130 cm
Musée d'Art Moderne,
Villeneuve d'Ascq,
France

Joan Prats, a fellow-student of Miró's in Barcelona and a lifelong friend, became a hatmaker. He built up an important collection of Miró's work and was also the publisher of the *Barcelona* series of lithographs at the end of the Second World War.

Miró has linked the photographs of hats (from Prats' own catalogue) and a 'Prats is quality' label with a comically sexual drawing. The face at the top is a caricature of Prats himself. Apart from the personal significance of the work, hats are symbols of respectability and of concealment ('keep it under your hat') and are perfect targets for a Surrealist joke such as this one. Miró seems to imply that beneath the very proper exterior of the prestigious premises in the Rambla Cataluña lay an impish sense of humour of which the customers were the chief victims.

Drawing-Collage (Homage to Prats)

63.3 x 47 cm
Fundacio Miró,
Barcelona

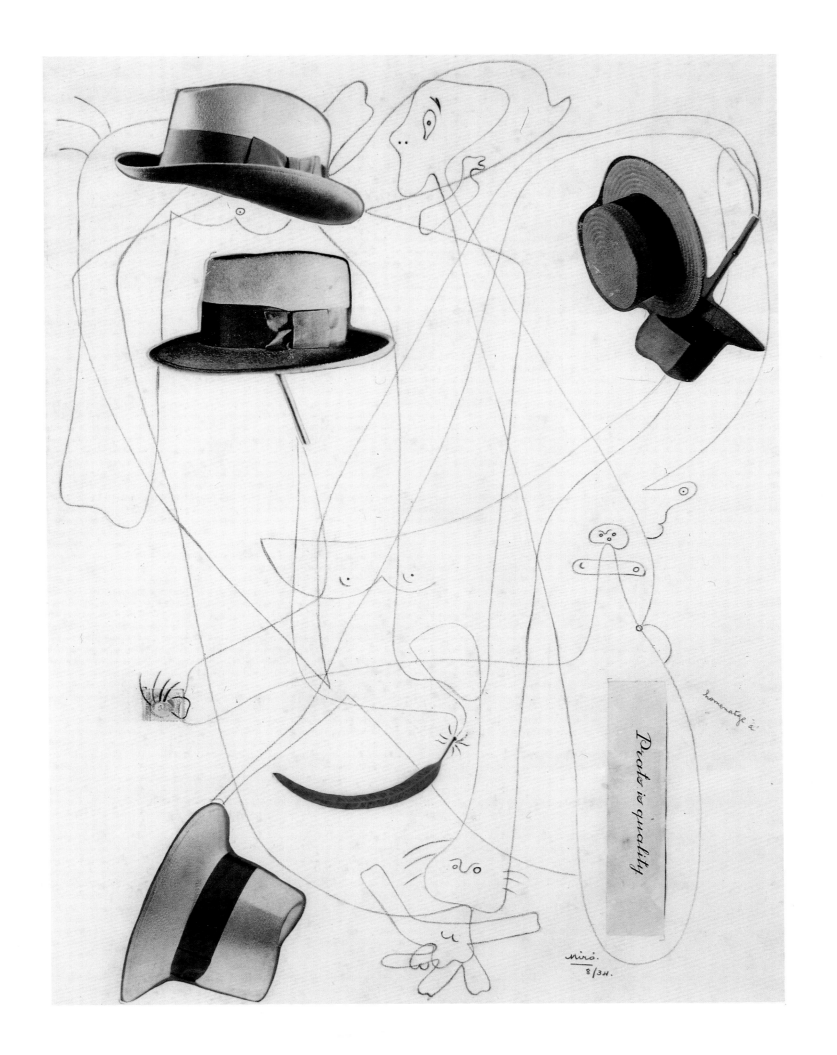

When Miró left Paris for Montroig in the summer of 1934 he was very aware of the growing political crisis in Spain, and the series of fifteen pictures he produced mark the first phase of the period which produced his 'savage paintings', in which his imagery expresses increasing anxiety and horror at the prospect and then the actuality of war.

In many of these pictures the barbarism of the period is reflected in the grotesque distortion of the human – often the female – form. This could not have been achieved using Miró's established 'sign language'; the processes which produced *Portrait of Mrs Mills in 1750* did not equip him for such vivid and horrific imagery. The world of the escape ladder was inaccessible. Instead, Miró uses the human form not as the starting point for calligraphic expression but, as if laid out on a butcher's slab, for the violent rearrangement of features and limbs.

As can he seen here, his colours intensified to give the new works added impact. The forms which were previously almost invariably unmodelled are henceforth shaded to strengthen their visual relationship to actual bodies. Here pastels have been used to give a range of acidic, almost fluorescent, colours which are heightened by the very dark background.

Woman, 1934

106 x 70 cm
Philadelphia Museum of Art

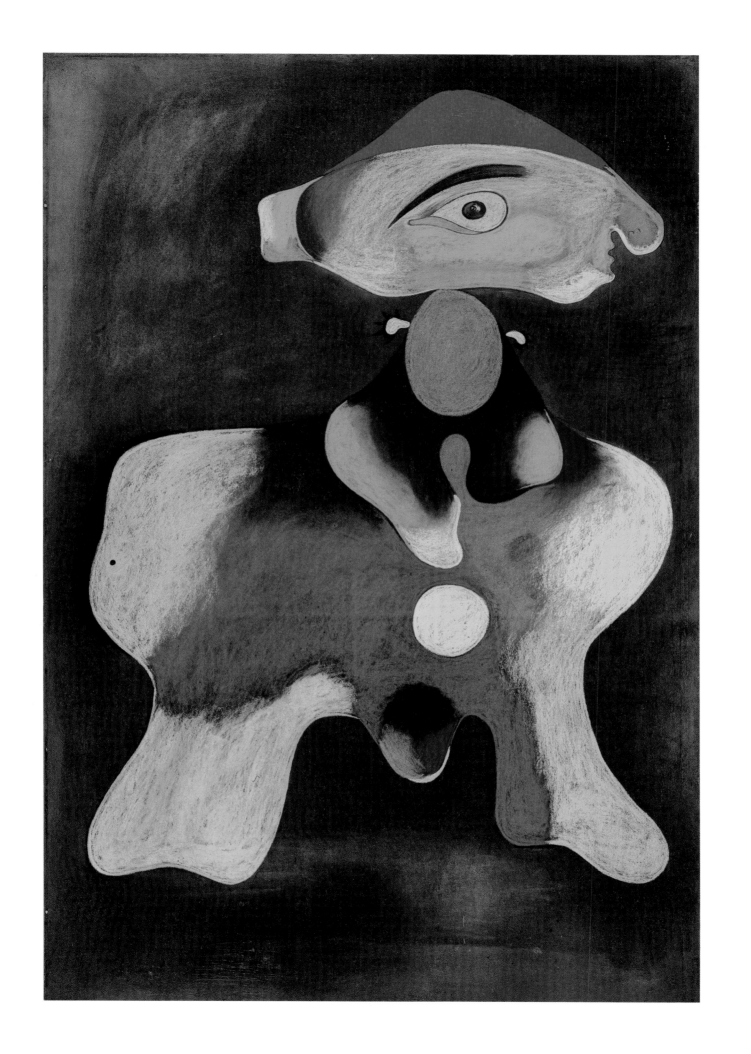

Although Miró was rarely politically active, his sympathies were very much with the Republican, left-wing faction in the Spanish Civil War. This poster was reproduced in stencilled form in the magazine *Cahiers d'Art*.

Although the Surrealists were by this time officially aligned to the Communist Party in France, Miró distrusted this development. As Georges Raillard points out, however, he did hold a view of art as a revolutionary force, stating that the '"plastic transformation" of painting implied in itself a transformation of ideas'*.

During the same year Miró produced a mural – his first large public work – for the Spanish Republican Government's pavilion at the International Exposition in Paris, a work assembled from several panels entitled *The Reaper* which is now sadly lost. Picasso's *Guernica* was displayed in the same building.

* Raillard, p 106

Aidez l'Espagne!
(Help Spain!), 1937
24.8 x 19.4 cm
Private collection

Dans la lutte actuelle, je vois du côté fasciste les forces
périmées, de l'autre côté le peuple dont les immenses ressources
créatrices donneront à l'Espagne un élan qui étonnera
le monde.   Miró.

Although it might easily be taken for an assemblage of 'found objects' casually and whimsically thrown together, this sculpture originated, like Miró's paintings, in a pencil sketch. The piece of wood, according to Raillard, is from a carob tree, the tree which dominated the farmyard at Montroig. This element is shaped rather like a foot, the swollen outsize foot visible in so many of his pictures which signifies the bond to the earth, and the tapping of its energy. But it is also the 'body' (literally, the trunk) of a figure, and an explicitly female body at that. The bedspring (which replaced a feather in the original conception) is reminiscent of the wire-like hair of *Portrait of Mrs Mills in 1750*, while the round metal shape implies a head, an eye, or perhaps the setting sun of the title, chained down.

The implications of the piece are complex; firstly, that the word 'object' is a pun, which could be rendered as the 'purpose' of the setting sun. Secondly, there is an equation of the female principle with the earth, as the foot-like body is drawn down in gravitational fashion, as the sun appears to be. Thirdly, the 'setting sun' may be a reference to the turn of political events.

Object of the Sunset, 1938

Musée National d'Art Moderne,
Paris

Suddenly, as the inevitability of war, or at least of an accommodation with Fascism sank in, Miró's art returned to the poeticism of the late 1920s, though now with an element of sentimentality which had previously been absent. As with so many of his images over the next seven years, this is a night-time scene. Darkness implies a threat, but in this period of Miró's life – marked by peril and uncertainty, both in France and back at home in Spain – the message of his pictures was that under the cover of this darkness life was continuing.

Although this is a poem-painting in the tradition of *This Is the Colour of My Dreams*, it also marked the beginning of a period in which long poetic phrases form the titles of paintings which include no written words, as in the next picture. Miró had rediscovered the escape ladder, and throughout the war his pictures seem to recount stories or bring news from a world which he upheld defiantly as better than reality. He knew better than anyone that it was this world, the realm of the imagination, that was under the greatest threat.

A Star Caresses the Breast
of a Black Woman, 1938
129.5 x 195 cm
Tate Gallery,
London

As the Germans invaded France Miró left Paris for the Normandy coast, renting a villa at Varengeville-sur-Mer, near the home of his close friend Georges Braque. Since he had been unable to remove most of his possessions from Paris, he had to make do with whatever materials he could find, and this picture is painted on sacking.

It is immediately apparent that he has hit upon a new way of deploying his language of signs. Oddly, and perhaps in both cases coincidentally, its ancestors seem to be *Homage to Prats* (page 99) and the *Object-Painting* (page 95) of 1931. In both of these the network is evident and in the *Homage* is produced by overlapping transparent forms to create new connexions between pictorial elements, as here. *Rosalie* opens out the enclosed masses of works like *Painting* (1933, page 97), using expressive lines to bind the composition (in a way which dimly recalls *Dutch Interior II*, page 87). The contrapuntal use of colour where forms intersect, for so long a feature of his work, is given a new dynamic by leaving many of the line-defined masses, and the background as a whole, entirely unpainted or only translucently shaded.

With this return to lyricism comes also a simplification of the relationship between painted sign and signified object; all the elements of the title are easily distinguishable in the image. Perhaps Miró had realized that if his work was to act, as he intended, as a transforming force, it would have to remain accessible to ordinary people.

Many writers have commented on the formal similarity between this period of Miró's work and the work of Paul Klee. Miró certainly had a deep admiration for Klee, and in addition there is a certain resemblance of themes between the artists' work. Klee also frequently painted or drew birds, flowers, stars, 'personages'; he was fond of night-scenes; his pictures often have musical and poetic overtones; he had a strong interest in colour theory. He was not directly involved with Surrealism, though sometimes his works were exhibited with those of the Surrealists. Miró was touched by the way the art of Paul Klee was driven underground in Nazi Germany.

A Drop of Dew Falling
from the Wing of a Bird
Awakens Rosalie Sleeping
in the Shadow of a Spider's Web,
1939

65 x 92 cm
University of Iowa Museum of Art

This series, begun in Varengeville and completed in Barcelona, occupied Miró totally for many months. The paintings were all based on laboriously produced drawings which were transferred precisely on to specially prepared paper. As can be seen from this selection, they divide into two basic types: complex interwoven images which are reminiscent of the star-charts from which the overall name of the series is derived, and – in contrast – very spare and simple images which have an atmosphere of greater space.

In the first (top left), *The Sunrise*, we can see a revision of the image of *Rosalie* (page 109), a female figure with arms raised surrounded by birds and stars and possessing a huge foot. The top of the 'escape ladder' is visible on the lower right of the picture. In *Numbers and Constellations in Love with a Woman* (lower right) this figure has been completely absorbed into her surroundings, interlaced with and penetrated by the cosmology of signs. She is accompanied by two smaller female personages, who appear to be threatening presences.

This undercurrent of threat, aptly summarized by Raillard as 'women-as-genitals, genital women, inhabiting a space somewhere between derision and anxiety'* is a hangover from the 'savage paintings'. A ferocious female presence is also visible in *Woman Encircled by the Flight of a Bird* (upper right). In *Women on the Beach* (based on a collage Miró had produced from an old postcard), the upper woman's body consists almost solely of the black-and-red sign for the vagina, a sign implied by the intersection of round forms in *Woman Encircled by the Flight of a Bird*. Clearly, despite the innocent playfulness of the titles and the delicate construction of these wartime images, Miró is still working within a language in which female sexuality is explicitly linked with themes of violence and anxiety. Again and again the objects surrounding female bodies are invasive, penetrative – even their own limbs seem to have been given an autosexual function, while their faces are often as suggestive of terror as they are of ecstasy.

*Raillard, p 112

Constellations, 1940-41

45 x 38 cm
Private collection

Miró was an inveterate collector of things which he felt might form the basis of a painting or sculpture or be useful in a collage; tram tickets, menu cards, broken appliances. His friend Prats was a great fan of the Barcelona flea-market, where he bought this mass-produced art nouveau (in Catalan 'moderniste') frame. When Miró saw it he asked to have it, and conceived this picture especially for it. The theme of figures under the night-time sky is typical of his wartime iconography, here incorporating delicate colours to complement the frame.

Painting with Moderniste Frame, 1943

40 x 30 cm
Fundacio Miró,
Barcelona

Although Miró had long desired to broaden his work into new media, his work in ceramics began almost by accident, though given his long friendship with Llorens 'Pepito' Artigas, the master-potter, it was probably inevitable. In Barcelona in 1944, Miró noticed a pile of broken pottery fragments in Artigas's studio, the results of a misfiring of the kiln. He asked for some, decorated them in enamel paint, and had them refired. They were exhibited with the *Constellations* series in New York immediately after the war.

Initially, the collaboration of Miró and Artigas was concentrated on the decoration of items such as pots, jugs and vases. Staying in the remote village of Gallifa (to which Artigas had moved at the beginning of the 1950s), Miró decorated some 200 objects during the summer of 1953. Gallifa replaced Montroig as a place of escape and contemplation for the next two decades, as Miró collaborated with Artigas and his son on an enormous quantity and range of ceramic works, including several huge murals for sites in the United States, France and Spain.

Apart from the permanence and brilliance of colour obtained in ceramic work, there is an element of luck and uncertainty created by fine differences in the materials used, the temperature of the kiln, impurities in the charcoal and so on, which greatly appealed to the artist.

Ceramic Plaque, 1946
*Collection J. Gardy
Artigas*

No better illustration could be found of Miró's unceasing experimentation than this extraordinary image, the title of which indicates not just what it is, but what it is about. For this is a big departure from the very carefully constructed, planned and executed works we have seem before. Here paint has been applied rapidly and in varying thicknesses to soak into the canvas, giving areas of more or less saturated colour. These have then suggested additional forms in his more usual, scrupulously flat technique, and he has added elements of collage.

Miró's immediate inspiration may have been his recent trip to the USA, and the impact of the nascent Abstract Expressionist painters, but there is a parallel with the manufacture of his *Constellations* series, in which scraped and washed paper produced a variable background which influenced the final drawing of these very complex images.

It is interesting that Miró did not pursue this technique for very long. Its effect is striking and almost three-dimensional, with the figurative signs seeming to hover in front of the dispersed colour fields of the background, and the collaged twine occupying a space somewhere between the two.

Painting, 1950

99 x 76 cm
Stedelijk Museum,
Eindhoven

From the 1950s Miró's work fractured into a multiplicity of broad 'styles', all drawing upon his established iconography, between which he seems to have moved according to his mood. Within his painting, three broad approaches are discernible; one, as here, utilized a very carefully controlled fine line, unvarying in thickness and texture, delineating areas of uniform colour. This style he adapted to most of his large-scale public works in ceramics. Secondly he sometimes adopted a freer technique, at times almost gestural (*Self-portrait 1937-60*, page 121; *Personage*, 1960, page 123). Thirdly, at times he painted in a style reminiscent of Japanese brush- or pen-work, with a more relaxed line (*Untitled*, 1967, page 125).

Although the forms are still linked, they are not linked as in some of the *Constellations* by a network which fills the entire picture space, but are a return to the simpler technique of the precursor of the *Constellations*, *Rosalie* (page 109) and of uncluttered images such as *Women on the Beach* (page 111). Areas within the forms are now patterned in a 'chequerboard' – a recent development, since contrasting colours divided by lines were in the past usually deployed where separate forms intersected, with as a general rule a single body being given a single colour. This may have been a result of his interest in ceramics, where large areas have to be filled with small facets, thereby making uniform colour difficult to achieve.

The Eagle Flies to the Peaks
of the Mountains Hollowed
Out by the Comets to Announce
the Words of the Poet, 1953

48 x 55 cm
Private collection

This may be unique in art – a double self-portrait with both the earlier and later images visible on the same canvas.

The 1937 self-portrait was made during the period of Miró's most violent and depressing imagery, yet it was a delicate and complex image of an artist with, literally, stars in his eyes, though with more threatening forms – a scissor-like bird's bill, thorns and teeth – around. In 1960 Miró made a copy in crayon (the squaring-up of the paper is visible here) and overlaid it with a rapid sign for himself and a few sparse touches of colour. The second image is contemporary with the *Blue* series, his most serene and largest canvases, whose small rotund bodies of colour echo the blue and black circles here.

Miró's 1960 self-image is part-caricature – the three strands of hair corresponding to his characteristic appearance with an unruly crown disrupting his otherwise neat hair. As befits a man whose name means 'the looker', it is an image of the unblinking, owlish gaze, the '*mirada fuerte*' or 'strong look' which was part of his folk heritage and the tradition of Catalan art (see page 9).

Self-portrait 1937-60

146.5 x 96.9 cm
Fundacio Miró,
Barcelona

Here Miró has inverted the arms of the 1960 *Self-portrait* and incorporated one of the roundels into the figures. The work is painted on a non-absorbent surface, with the white paint applied first and the drawing scratched into it with a brush-handle. The black paint was applied when this had dried.

To all appearances a placid man, Miró often spoke of the violence which he felt when working, a violence which he said increased as he grew older. His visits to the USA encouraged him to work from time to time directly in paint, without preparatory drawings, but he was too concerned with the external object, with meticulous description and lengthy contemplation, to make this method anything but occasionally attractive. There is a strong suggestion of catharsis here, just as with the *Self-portrait 1937-60*. Here the violence is gestural; there it is also present in the apparent 'vandalism' and implicit rejection of the earlier version.

Personage, 1960

105 x 75 cm
Pierre Matisse Gallery,
New York

Miró's interest in oriental painting is nowhere more apparent than in this image, whose calligraphy deliberately mimics Sino-Japanese script and whose central feature, the red sun, though a long-standing part of his repertoire, is the national symbol of Japan.

His interest extended to oriental poetry, and in particular to the seventeen-syllable Japanese form called *haiku*, the tone of which he often attempted to capture in his own poetic titles. This is close to a visual equivalent of this most minimal and precise, yet most suggestive, poetic form. The single star, the 'escape ladder', a sinuous trail suggesting the flight of a bird and the rising sun are an iconography pared down into a simple, yet immensely expressive image.

Miró's choice of materials here, ink and watercolour on very thin paper, also indicates a deliberate attempt to bring to his work the flavour of Japanese art.

Untitled, 1967

34.5 x 50 cm
Artcurial Collection,
Paris

A series of sketches in the Fundacio Miró indicate that, as with the previous image, in 1967 Miró was preoccupied with expressing the idea of a moment at dawn; a moment in which, as his notes say, '[a] Bird awakened by a shrill cry...[has] flown away...over the rolling plain.' Since his early days at Montroig he had been fascinated by the flight of birds, the invisible lines they traced and the mysterious 'signs' and formations created by flocks. He felt that they were somehow significant, part of a hidden language of nature waiting to be translated.

In *The Gold of the Azure*, as in *Untitled* (page 125), Miró celebrates this moment and the first flight of the waking bird. The blue form, created with rapid tight swirls of a small brush, takes the place of the red sun – indeed, he has simply given the 'sky' the sun's colour and the 'sun' that of the heavens – but it also suggests other things, perhaps a body of water or a cloud as in *The Siesta* (page 77). Across this is traced the line of the bird's flight while a gravid, very earthbound female form looks on, echoing a 'constellation' on the right. The long black crescent appears to be a distant echo of the encircling arm visible in *Dutch Interior II* (page 87), and certainly of the upraised arms of the figure on the left; we may take them to signify an embrace in a metaphorical sense.

The Gold of the Azure, 1967

205 x 173.5 cm
Fundacio Miró,
Barcelona

Having first worked in bronze in 1944, Miró had only intermittently employed the technique, although given his craftsmanship and strong tactile sense, he was fascinated by the transformatory process.

As an image, it appears quite untypical of Miró's output; though clock imagery is present in *The Siesta* (page 77), his work rarely if ever refers to the Dada tradition of playful pseudo-machinery or even focuses on a single object before this point. Machine diagrams did interest him, but they were the basis of a transformation into pseudo-organic forms, as in *Queen Louise of Prussia* (page 87). At first glance the strongest point of reference is simply that of a round form encompassed by a square, framing one, as in a painting, but here the spoon/hand erupts through this encasement, and gradually one sees resemblances and echoes elsewhere. The angle of this feature, its suggestion of movement and escape, are all reminiscent of a classic Miró sign, that of the cockerel visible in *The Tilled Field* (page 61), *The Carnival of Harlequin* (page 71), and many other paintings where it resembles nothing more strongly than a weather-vane or 'wind-clock'. Even closer is the residual sign for the carob tree found in *Catalan Landscape (The Hunter)* (page 73), the single branch and leaf of which intersect with a circular form in precisely this way.

The Wind Clock, 1967

51 x 29.5 x 16 cm
Fundacio Miró,
Barcelona

The blue form of *The Gold of the Azure* is here confirmed as signifying both sun and sky simultaneously. That picture dealt with movement, as did its precursor, *Untitled* (page 125). Here everything is still, the only 'motion' being the recognition of one form, the star, of its 'twin', the tree, and thus of the movement of our own eyes and minds as we make this poetic connexion. But there is also a latent movement, a precarious balance, in its composition. Apart from its extreme simplicity – even the background has been left unpainted – the most remarkable feature of this canvas is the deployment of signs in the upper left corner, with the line of the horizon, the 'plain', ending abruptly three-quarters of the way across. The effect of this can best be realized by mentally completing the rest of the line to the frame; immediately the image becomes static, losing the sense of vertigo engendered by the undefined space on the right.

What Miró has done, therefore, is to invest what would otherwise have risked being a banal composition with a sense of unease, producing, by artificial means, an effect which signifies the 'shock' – a word he often used to indicate a sudden poetic understanding or recognition of an object – which he himself experienced when encountering the relationship between the tree and the star.

The Smile of the Star to the Twin Tree of the Plain, 1968

174 x 217 cm
Suzy and Daniel Lelong collection,
Paris

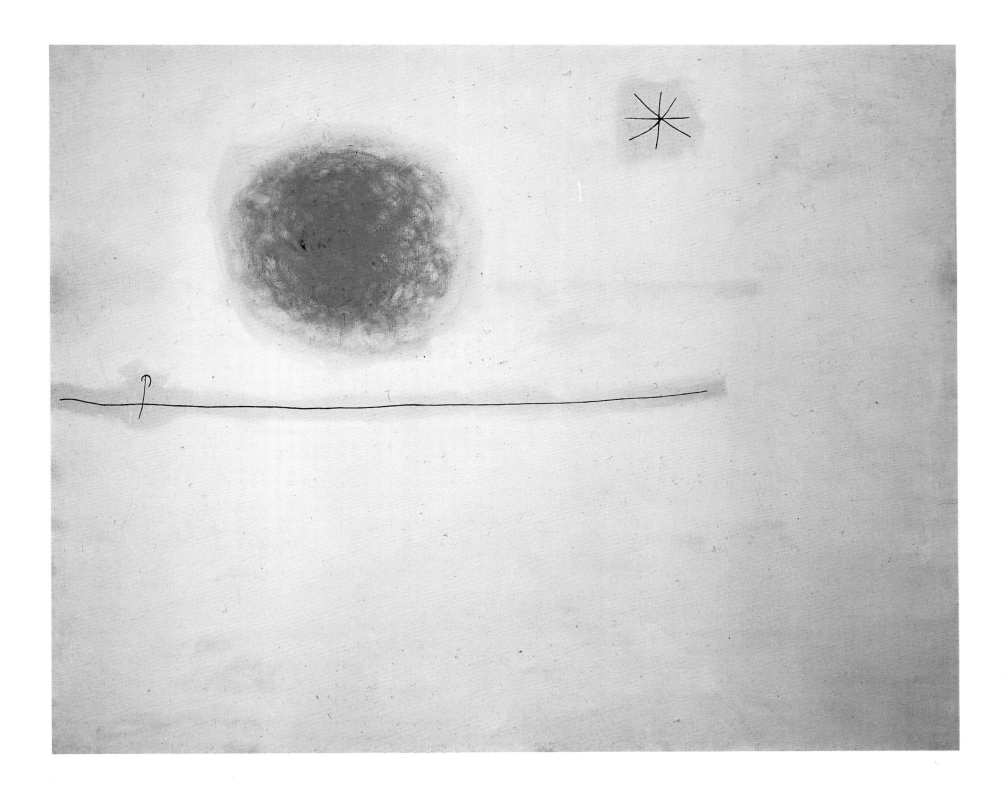

In large-scale sculptures, Miró found what he regarded as the supreme achievement of his or any other's art, the ability to place his work in 'real space', to make it truly part of the world. His frequent acceptance of commissions for public spaces and buildings reflects his often-voiced desire that his art should speak directly to the broad mass of people, and not be confined to museums and galleries.

One of Miró's favourite places, and one which had a lasting influence on his art, was the Guell Park in Barcelona, designed by the great Catalan architect Antoni Gaudí. Miró spent many hours there as a youth, studying the art nouveau buildings, benches and fixtures, delighted by the transformation of the real world into an exotic, multicoloured, dream-like environment. When in the early 1960s Miró was commissioned to design a sculpture-garden for the foundation set up by his dealer at Saint-Paul-de-Vence he had the opportunity to create his own world-within-a-world. Besides decorating the surrounding walls and existing buildings with sculpted and ceramic plaques, he made the central feature of the garden a labyrinth, in which he placed a series of monumental sculptures – *The Egg*, *The Lizard*, *The Goddess* – in a physical journey through the iconography of his art, the world that exists at the top of the escape ladder.

The *Lunar Bird* is an inhabitant who appears in the night-world of the *Constellations*, whose sculptural form expresses the cry which Miró often referred to in the notes for and titles of his works. Although the lunar form can be seen on the creature's head, it is an entirely earthbound being, weighed down by its massive 'legs', and has arms rather than wings. It is not on the moon but crying up at it, and its iconography is not that of a bird, but of the female humanoid forms which populate Miró's canvases – *Rosalie* (page 109) and *The Sunrise* (page 111), for example.

Lunar Bird, 1968

300 x 260 x 120 cm
Maeght Foundation,
Saint-Paul-de-Vence,
France

This is a rare direct reference to a real political event (perhaps the first since his lost painting for the Republican Pavilion at the Paris Exposition in 1937, *The Reaper*). The time-lapse between the student rebellion and the date of this painting may be explained by Miró's practice of putting aside canvases for several months or even years before completing them. There is a suggestion here of the interplay of several coexistent techniques, variously calm and animated.

Miró's sympathies in 1968 were very much on the side of the students, though his political consciousness, at least of events outside Spain, was perhaps not much more focused than were the demands of the students themselves. Yet the moment seemed to be one of potential transformation, of the revolution in thinking, in attitudes and in perceptions which Miró, even if chiefly through his painting and only rarely through direct action, had been seeking all his life. Certainly the Surrealists were heroes to many of the young radicals of the 1960s, not least because of the perceived relationship between much Surrealist imagery and the experience of 'consciousness-expanding' or hallucinogenic drugs, but also because of the explicit commitment of Breton's group to the overthrow of capitalism.

May 1968 contains that rarity in Miró's imagery, a direct sign for part of the human body, without any transformation; in this case, the handprint. With the thrown black paint signifying the brutal suppression of the student rebellion by the state, the handprints, since they are also black, imply actual physical blows. Alternatively they can be read as struggling against the oppressive force, trying to hold it back. The final image is one of delicate, colourful forms invaded by fanged and clawed predatory ones, of a new world from which we have been cut off by the barbed wire of interlaced black lines.

May 1968, 1973

200 x 200 cm
Fundacio Miró,
Barcelona

The violent imagery of *May 1968*, a direct political protest, is here extended into an act of violence against the work, and the world, of art. 'I will smash their guitars' Miró once said of the Cubists – violence haunts his entire career. He has no affection for the commercial realities of the art world, its hype or its élitism, and four years earlier had at an exhibition in Barcelona deliberately wiped out the paintings he had created on the windows of the gallery to prevent them from being preserved and sold commercially. 'I am not a meal to be eaten,' he protested in the context of the 'borrowing' of his imagery by the world of commercial design.*

But the Burnt Canvases were not merely a gesture of defiance. They represent a logical extension of the search in his art for a revolution in perception, the forcing of the viewer into acceptance of the truth, the reality of what he or she sees. In this, the Burnt Canvases are closely related to *This Is the Colour of My Dreams* (page 79). What is there presented as a statement of fact, a 'Photo' – that this is how things are despite the fact that you are looking at a painting – is here represented with almost heavy-handed literality. We look through the painting at reality. The canvas is opened up, a space in which anything can appear.

There is a third dimension to these extraordinary works, one which given Miró's insistence on the 'Catalan' nature of his art and his thought we should be careful to consider. Raillard makes the point that it is a Catalan custom on St John's Eve to make a bonfire of everything you no longer want, a kind of ritual cleansing, deliberately closing off one's former life. When Miró moved to Mallorca he did this with a single-mindedness and courage few artists could achieve, destroying hundreds of his works. There may certainly be a sense, then, in which the Burnt Canvases mark the disavowal of part of his own œuvre, or at the very least a sense of frustration at the limitations imposed upon his ability to express himself by the physical confines of paint and canvas.

* Raillard, p 138

Burnt Canvas I, 1973

130.5 x 194.6 cm
Fundacio Miró,
Barcelona

'Some years ago, on a large canvas, I had painted a little white line; on another canvas I painted a blue line. And then one day it all came to me... it was when that poor Catalan boy, Salvador Puig Antich, was garrotted. I had a feeling it was that, the day he was killed. I finished the canvas on that day, without knowing he was dead. A line which was going to be interrupted. It was not an intellectual coincidence, but a magical coincidence. I don't know exactly how to express it.'*

Salvador Puig Antich was a young Catalan nationalist executed in one of the final acts of political violence of the Franco regime. The imagery, of the sun in three stages marking the passing of the day, the final day, is that of several earlier canvases, though the celebration of these earlier works is replaced here by a kind of enervation, a sense of distance from the objects, which we seem to be viewing through a mist. Despite the sense of sadness engendered by the title and the anecdotal evidence of their production, they remain supremely beautiful images; as metaphysical landscapes they stand alongside those of Turner or Van Gogh.

* Miró, quoted in Raillard's *This Is the Colour of My Dreams* here translated by Olga Grlic.

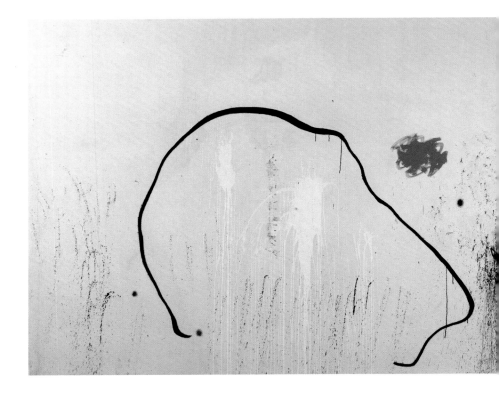

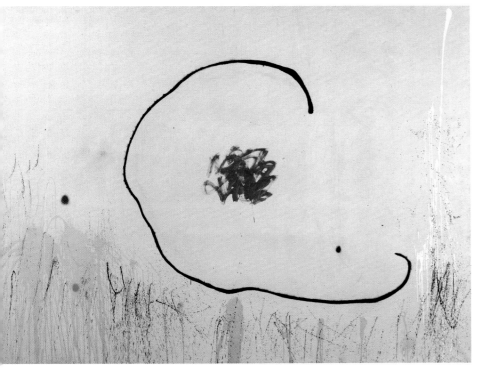

Triptych for the Cell of
a Condemned Man, 1974

I: 267.3 x 351.5 cm
II: 267.3 x 351 cm
III: 267 x 350.3 cm
Fundacio Miró,
Barcelona

CHRONOLOGY

1893 April 20th, 9pm: Joan Miró Ferra born at No 4 Passatge del Credit, Barcelona.

1900 Begins school in the Carrer de Regomir. First drawing lessons, with Señor Civil. Summer holidays with father's parents in Cornudella, Tarragona, and mother's family in Palma, Mallorca.

1901 First surviving drawing, of interior of a chiropodist's.

1907 Begins business classes at insistence of his father, and art instruction at the 'Llotja', the main Barcelona art school.

1910 Works as a book-keeper. The family buys a farm at Montroig which becomes Miró's spiritual home.

1911 Falls ill, probably a psychosomatic reaction to deep depression. His father gives up hope of persuading him to remain in business. He decides to become a full-time painter.

1912 Miró begins classes at the private art school of Francesc Gali. Begins lifelong friendships with Josep Llorens Artigas, Enric Ricart Nin and Josep Rafols Fontanals.

c.1913-1914 Enrols in drawing lessons with the Cercle Artistic de Sant Lluc. Meets Joan Prats. Shows three paintings in a Sant Lluc exhibition. Rents a studio with Enric Ricart.

1915 Military conscription, October to December.

1916 Meets art dealer Josep Dalmau. Probably sees Dadaist literature for the first time. Visits French art exhibition in Barcelona organized by Parisian dealer Ambroise Vollard. Another three months' military service. Meets Francis Picabia, Dadaist painter and poet and international playboy, through Dalmau.

1917 Reads poetry of Guillaume Apollinaire. Paintings: *Nord-Sud; Hermitage de Sant Joan d'Horta; The Church at Ciurana; Prades; Portrait of E. C. Ricart; Portrait of J. F. Rafols.*

1918 First one-man show of 64 paintings and drawings, at Dalmau's Gallery (18 Carrer de la Portaferrissa). Co-founds an artistic group, with Llorens Artigas, the Agrupacio Courbet (Courbet Group). Paintings: *Still Life with Coffee Mill; H Casany; Juanita Obrador; R Sunyer; Little Girl; The House with the Palm Tree; The Kitchen Garden with Donkey.*

1919-20 First Paris visit. Attends a Dada event at the Salle Gaveau. Agrupacio Courbet exhibition, Barcelona. Paintings: *Montroig, the Church and Village; Vineyards and Olive-groves at Montroig; Self-portrait; Nude with Looking-glass. Self-portrait* is given to Picasso.

1920 Spends summer in Montroig. In Barcelona Dalmau's exhibition *Avant-garde French Art* [sic] includes three of Miró's works alongside others by Picasso, Severini, Signac, Dufy, Matisse, Laurencin, Gris, Braque etc. Painting: *The Table.*

1921 Returns to Paris. Associates with Masson, Leiris, Limbour, Salacrou, Tual. Miró's first one-man Paris show is organized by Dalmau, at Galerie La Licorne. Summer in Montroig. Paintings: *Portrait of a Spanish Dancer; Standing Nude;* begins *The Farm.*

1922 November - December *The Farm* is shown at the Salon d'Automne. Paintings: *The Farmer's Wife; Flowers and Butterfly.*

1923 Exhibits at Salon d'Automne. Meets Hemingway, Pound, Henry Miller, Jacques Prévert. Summer at Montroig. Paintings: *The Tilled Field; Earth; Pastorale; Catalan Landscape (The Hunter).*

1924 First Surrealist Manifesto published. Summer in Montroig. Paintings: *Portrait of Señora K; Maternity; The Bottle of Wine; The Carnival of Harlequin.*

1925 One-man show at Galerie Pierre (Loeb) 'very successful'. Sees Klee's work. November: included in *La Peinture surréaliste* exhibition at Galerie Pierre. First 'dream painting' and 'poem painting'. Paintings: *The Dialogue of Insects; Head of a Catalan Peasant; Le corps de ma brune* (poem painting).

1926 Works on set of *Romeo and Juliet* with Max Ernst. Miró's father dies. Miró has two paintings in International Modern Art exhibition in Brooklyn, New York. Paintings: *Dog Howling at the Moon; Horse on the Seashore; Character Throwing a Stone at a Bird.*

1927 Moves to rue Tourlaque, Montmartre (Cité des Fusains); neighbours Ernst, Jean Arp, Magritte, Bonnard. Paintings: 'circus' scenes and compositions with white backgrounds.

1928 Trips to Netherlands and Belgium. Exhibition at Galerie Georges Bernheim, Paris, his breakthrough. First trip to Madrid. Meets Alexander Calder. Paintings: paintings from postcards; first collages; *Dutch Interior I, II & III; The Potato.*

1929 October12th: Marries Pilar Juncosa in Palma, Mallorca. On return to Paris moves to 3 rue François Mouthon. Paintings: *Queen Louise of Prussia, Portrait of Mrs Mills in 1750; La Fornarina.*

1930 Several one-man shows in Paris. Included in *La peinture au défi* at Galerie Goemans, Brussels. First US one-man show, Valentine Gallery, NY. First lithographs for Tzara's *L'Arbre des voyageurs.* Meets dealer Pierre Matisse.

1931 July 17th: Birth of his daughter, Maria Dolores, in Barcelona. Exhibition of object-sculptures, Galerie Pierre. Exhibition at Chicago Art Club.

1932 Moves back to Barcelona. Designs costumes, decor and sets for *Jeux d'enfants.* Exhibitions at Galerie Pierre, Paris and Pierre Matisse Gallery, New York, and with Surrealist group.

1933 May 3rd: *Jeux d'enfants* opens in Barcelona. Meets Wassily Kandinsky. First etchings. Exhibiton at Galerie Bernheim, Paris, of large-format paintings from collages. First London exhibition.

1934 Living in Barcelona. Large-scale 'savage' works in pastel and on sandpaper and other textured surfaces. Painting: *Snail, Woman, Flower, Star; Swallow of Love*.

1935 Living in Barcelona. Takes part in Surrealist exhibition in Tenerife, Lucerne and Copenhagen. Executes 'savage paintings'.

1936 Outbreak of Spanish Civil War. Visits London and Paris, where he remains due to events in Spain. Included in *L'art contemporain* exhibition, Paris. Included in *Fantastic Art, Dada, Surrealism* exhibition at MOMA, New York. First monograph on Miró published (in Japanese) by Shuzo Takiguchi. Paints on fibrocement, and in tempera, and on copper plates. *Construction*.

1937 Paints *The Reaper* (lost) for Spanish Republican Government Pavilion, Paris World Fair. Designs poster *Aidez l'Espagne!* for *Cahiers d'Art*. Painting: *Still Life with Old Shoe*.

1938 Spends summer at Varengeville-sur-Mer, Normandy. In Surrealist exhibition, Galerie des Beaux Arts, Paris. Painting: *A Star Caresses the Breast of a Black Woman*.

1939 January: Franco occupies Barcelona. Settles in Varengeville. Paints on hessian/sackcloth. Preparatory drawings for *Barcelona* series of lithographs (1944) on report paper.

1940 January 20th: Begins *Constéllations* series (23 gouaches). Finishes *Constéllations* in Mallorca in September.

1941 First large retrospective, MOMA New York, organized by James Johnson Sweeney, who writes first major English-language monograph on Miró.

1942 Returns to Barcelona. Paintings on paper.

1944 Mother dies. Begins to work in ceramics with Llorens Artigas. First bronzes. Printing of 50 lithographs of *Barcelona* series.

1945 Exhibition *Ceramics and Constellations*, Pierre Matisse Gallery, New York. Works on terracotta sculptures and series of paintings on white and black surfaces.

1946 *Four Spaniards* exhibition in Boston.

1947 First visit to USA. Makes 10x3m mural for Cincinnati Terrace Plaza (Hilton) Hotel. Takes part in Surrealist exhibition at Galerie Maeght, Paris.

1948 Returns to Paris from USA. Exhibition at Galerie Maeght. Painting: *The Red Sun Gnaws at the Spider*.

1949 Exhibition of 57 works from Barcelona collections at Galeries Laietanes, Barcelona. Retrospective in Kunsthalle, Bern.

1950 First woodcuts. Paints mural for Harkness Graduate Center, Harvard, commissioned by Walter Gropius and Josep Sert.

1952 Miró visits Paris and sees Jackson Pollock exhibition. Miró

retrospective in Kunsthalle, Basle. Large number of canvases in a freer, more active style.

1953 Starts work in Gallifa with Llorens Artigas on 200 ceramic objects. Exhibition in Bern.

1954 Grand Prize for graphic work, Venice Biennalle. Gives up painting, except for a small series in 1955, until 1959.

1955 Invited to decorate two walls at UNESCO building, Paris. Included in *documenta 1*, Kassel. Small paintings on cardboard.

1956 Moves to Palma. Begins work on ceramic murals for UNESCO building (*Wall of the Sun; Wall of the Moon*). Exhibition of the *Terres de grand feu* at Galerie Maeght, Paris and Pierre Matisse Gallery, NY. Retrospectives in Brussels, Amsterdam, Basle.

1958 Completes UNESCO commission.

1959 Retrospectives in New York and Los Angeles. Second trip to United States. May 18th: receives Guggenheim Award (Grand Prix) for UNESCO work. Included in *documenta II*, Kassel.

1960 Artigas and Miró work on ceramic mural to replace painting on Harvard Graduate Center wall. Mural shown in Barcelona, Paris and New York before installation.

1961 Visits the USA for third time. Exhibitions at Galerie Maeght and Pierre Matisse Gallery. Graphic exhibition in Geneva. Painting: the triptych *Blue I-II-III*.

1962 Exhibition of 250 works at Musée National d'Art Moderne, Paris. Creation of Joan Miró Prize for Drawing in Barcelona.

1964 Inauguration of Fondation Maeght, Saint-Paul-de-Vence. With Artigas produces ceramic mural for Ecole supérieure, St Gall, Switzerland. Major retrospective at Tate Gallery, London and Kunsthaus, Zurich. Included in *documenta III*, Kassel.

1965 Exhibition at Pierre Matisse Gallery. Cover for Catalan children's magazine *Cavall Fort*.

1966 Artigas and Miró produce underwater ceramic sculpture *Venus of the Sea*, Juan-les-Pins, France. Retrospective at National Museum of Modern Art, Tokyo, and in Kyoto. First trip to Japan. First monumental bronze sculptures. Painting: *The Skiing Lesson*.

1967 Carnegie Prize for Painting. Bronze sculptures based on found objects. Painting: *The Gold of the Azure*.

1968 City authorities in Barcelona stage 'The Year of Miró'. Honorary degree, Harvard University. Fifth and last trip to the USA. Large retrospective at Maeght Foundation, Saint-Paul-de-Vence. Included in *Dada, Surrealism and their Heritage* exhibition, New York, Chicago and Los Angeles.

1969 *Miró otro* (The Other Miró) exhibition at Architectural Association of Cataluña, Barcelona. Paintings on glass destroyed by Miró at close of show.

1970 Large ceramic mural with Artigas at Barcelona Airport. Three monumental ceramic murals and water garden for the Glass Pavilion, World's Fair (International Exhibition), Osaka.

1971-72 Exhibition of sculpture, Art Institute of Chicago, tours Cleveland, Boston, Minneapolis, Hayward Gallery, London and Kunsthaus, Zurich.

1972 Fundacio Joan Miró created.

1973 'Overweaves' exhibited at Galerie Maeght. Burnt canvases. Numerous honours to celebrate his 80th birthday.

1974 Painting, sculpture and ceramics exhibition of c350 exhibits at Grand Palais, Paris. Graphics exhibition at Musée d'Art Moderne. Painting: *Triptych for the Cell of a Condemned Man*.

1975 10th June: Unofficial opening of Fundacio Miró Centre d'Estudis d'Art Contemporani, Montjuic Park, Barcelona. Death of General Franco. Major retrospective at Galeria Maeght.

1976 Exhibition of small-scale ceramic and graphic work at Galeria Mas, Madrid. June 18th: Official opening of Fundacio Miró. Exhibition of 475 drawings from almost 5,000 donated to the foundation by Miró, dating from 1901 onwards.

1977 Graphics exhibition at Centre de Lectura, Reus. Collaborated on a production of Jarry's *Ubu Roi*. Exhibition of painting, sculpture and graphics at the Museum of Ceret, France. Ceramic work for University of Wichita, Kansas. Tapestry in conjunction with Josep Royo for National Art Gallery, Washington.

1978 Fundacio Miró receives Special Prize for museums from Council of Europe. Catalan theatre piece *Mori el Merma* tours Europe. Retrospectives in Madrid and Mallorca. Print retrospective, Madrid. Exhibitions of drawings (Centre Georges Pompidou), and *100 sculptures* (Musée d'Art Moderne) in Paris. Monumental sculpture for La Défense, Paris. Major exhibition of recent work (1969-78) at Pierre Matisse Gallery, NY.

1979 Exhibition of drawings, Hayward Gallery, London. Retrospective of paintings at Orsanmichele, Florence. Graphics exhibition, Siena. Major retrospective at Maeght Foundation. Included in *Homenatge a Gaudí* exhibition at Galerie Maeght, Barcelona. Designs windows for church of Saint-Frambourg, Senlis, and tapestry for Fundacio Miró.

1980 Exhibition: *Joan Miró: The Development of a Sign Language* at Washington University Gallery of Art, St Louis, Missouri, and in Chicago. Retrospective exhibitions at Washington, Mexico City and Caracas. Ceramic mural for Palacio de Congreso y Expositiones, Madrid. Travelling exhibition in Japan.

1981 Unveiling of monumental sculpture *Miss Chicago* in Chicago. Costume and set designs for ballet *Miró l'Ucello Luce*, Venice.

Unveiling of two monumental sculptures, Palma de Mallorca. Huge retrospective in various locations in Milan.

1982 Unveiling of monumental sculpture *Personage and Bird*, Houston, Texas, at Miró in America exhibition. Retrospective exhibition, Fundacio Joan Miró, Barcelona. Unveiling of monumental sculpture *Dona i Ocell* in new park on site of former slaughterhouse in Barcelona.

1983 Unveiling of monumental sculpture in patio of government building, Barcelona. Miró dies, aged 90, on Christmas Day in Palma. Buried in Montjuic cemetery, Barcelona.

SELECT BIBLIOGRAPHY

ALEXANDRIAN, Sarane   *Surrealist Art*, London; Thames & Hudson.
BERNIER, Rosamond   *Matisse, Picasso, Miró As I Knew Them*, London; Sinclair-Stevenson 1991.
BRETON, André,   *Le Surréalisme et la Peinture*, Paris; Gallimard 1928.
BUCCI, Mario   *Miró*, London; Hamlyn 1970.
DUPIN, Jacques   *Miró*, Paris; Flammarion 1961.
DUPIN, Jacques   *Miró: Life and Work*, London; Thames and Hudson/New York; Abrams 1962.
ERBEN, Walter   *Miró: The Man and his Work*, Köln: Benedikt Taschen 1993.
ERBEN, Walter   *Miró*, Munich; Prestel Verlag 1959.
FONDACION MIRÓ   *Obra de Joan Miró*, Barcelona 1988.
GRLIC, Olga   unpublished material appended to, and a translation of Raillard, *Miró* (see below).
HUGHES, Robert   *Barcelona*, London; Harvill 1992.
HUNTER, Sam   *Miró: das grafisches Werk*, Munich; Prestel Verlag 1958.
JEAN, Marcel & MEZEI, Arpad   *A History of Surrealist Painting*, London; Weidenfeld & Nicolson 1967.
MALET, Rosa Maria   *Miró*, Barcelona; Ediciones Poligrafa 1983/London; Academy Editions 1988.
MINK, Janis   *Miró*, Köln; Benedikt Taschen 1993.
NADEAU, Maurice   *The History of Surrealism*, Penguin; Harmondsworth.
PENROSE, Roland   *Miró*, London; Thames and Hudson 1970.
RAILLARD, Georges   *Miró*, Paris; Editions Hazan /London; Studio Editions 1989.
RAILLARD, Georges   *Ceci est la Couleur de mes Rêves*, Paris.
RICHARDSON, John   *A Life of Picasso, Volume 1*. London; Jonathan Cape 1991.
ROWELL, Margit, ed   *Joan Miró: Selected Writings and Interviews*, London; Thames and Hudson 1987.
SOBY, James Thrall   *Joan Miró*, New York; Museum of Modern Art 1959.
SWEENEY, James Johnson   *Joan Miró*, New York; Museum of Modern Art 1941.
SYLVESTER, David   *Dada & Surrealism* (catalogue), London; Hayward Gallery 1975.

WALDBERG, Patrick *Surrealism*, London, Thames and Hudson nd.
WEELEN, Guy *Miró*, Paris; Editions Hazan 1961.

LIST OF ILLUSTRATIONS

All works are by Miró unless otherwise stated

Frontispiece: *Miró working on a poster for the exhibition* Agora 1, 1971. Museum of Modern Art, Strasbourg. Photo: Archives Succession Miró.

7 *The Pedicure*, 1901. Pencil, watercolour and ink on paper. 11.6 x 11.7 cm. Fundacio Miró, Barcelona.

8 Parque Guell. Antoni Gaudí. Photo: AISA.

11 *Virgin with Child*. Detail of a mural in the nave of the Church of San Pedro de Sorpe, *c.* 1125. The Museum of Art, Cataluña. Photo: AISA.

15 *Self-portrait*, 1919. Oil on canvas. 73 x 60 cm. Musée Picasso, Paris. Gift of Picasso. Photo: Réunion des Musées Nationaux.

16 *Montroig: The Church and Village*, 1919. Oil on canvas. 73 x 61 cm. Dolores Miró de Punyet Collection. Photo: AISA.

19 *Table with Glove*, 1921. Oil on canvas. 116.8 x 89.5 cm. The Museum of Modern Art, New York. Gift of Armand G. Erpf.

23 *Maternity*, 1924. Oil on canvas. 91 x 74 cm. Scottish National Gallery of Modern Art, Edinburgh.

27 Preparatory Collage for *Painting*, 1933. Pencil and collage on paper. 47.1 x 63.1 cm. Fundacio Miró, Barcelona.

28 Marcel Duchamp *Nude Descending a Staircase no 2*, 1920. Oil on canvas. 147.3 x 88.9 cm. Philadelphia Museum of Art: The Louise and Walter Arensberg Collection.© ADAGP, Paris and DACS, London 1995.

29 *Nude Woman Climbing a Staircase*, 1937. Pencil on paper. 78 x 50 cm. Fundacio Miró, Barcelona.

31 Stage set for *Jeux d'enfants*, 1932. Fundacio Miró, Barcelona.

32 *Etoile, nichons, escargots*, 1937. Poem drawing, 75 x 105 cm Musée National d'Art Moderne, Centre Georges Pompidou, Paris.

33 Verso of the plate *The Morning Star from Constellations*. New York 1959. Dept des imprimés, Bibliothèque Nationale, Paris.

34 Poster for the exhibition at the Maeght Gallery, 1948. Colour lithograph. 65 x 50 cm. Photo: Fundacio Miró, Barcelona.

38 *La Fourche* 1963 et *Labyrinthe Miró Céramique Ronde* 1973. The Maeght Foundation. Saint Paul de Vence. Photo: Claude Germain/Fundacio Miró, Barcelona.

40 *Letter and Numbers Attracted by a Spark*, 1968. Oil on canvas. 146 x 114 cm. Photo: Fundacio Miró, Barcelona

42 Man Ray, *Photograph of Miró*(detail), 1934 © ADAGP, Paris and DACS, London 1995.

45 *The Beach at Montroig*, 1916. Oil on canvas. 37.3 x 45.6 cm. Fundacio Miró, Barcelona. Photo: Fundacio Miró, Barcelona

47 *Nord-Sud 1917*. Oil on canvas. 62 x 70 cm. Adrien Maeght, Paris. Photo: Archives Succession Miró.

49 *The Church at Ciurana* 1917. Oil on canvas. 46 x 55 cm. Private Collection. Photo: Archives Succession Miró.

51 *Portrait of E. C. Ricart*, 1917. Oil and print glued to canvas. 81 x 65 cm. Metropolitan Museum of Art, New York.

53 *Standing Female Nude*, 1918. Oil on canvas. 152 x 122 cm. The Saint Louis Art Museum.

55 *The Kitchen Garden with Donkey*, 1918. Oil on canvas. 60 x 70 cm. Moderna Museet, Stockholm.

57 *Portrait of a Young Girl*, 1919. Oil on paper. 33 x 28 cm. Fundacio Miró, Barcelona.

59 *The Farm*, 1921–22. Oil on canvas. 132 x 147 cm. National Gallery of Art, Washington.

61 *The Tilled Field*, 1923. Oil on canvas. 66 x 94 cm. The Solomon R. Guggenheim Museum, New York. Photo: David Heald. ©The Solomon R. Guggenheim Foundation, New York.

63 *Catalan Landscape (The Hunter)*, 1923–24. Oil on canvas. 64.8 x 100.3 cm. Museum of Modern Art, New York.

65 *The Wind*, 1924. Watercolour, black crayon and collage on paper. 60 x 46.4 cm. Acquavella Galleries, New York.

67 *My Blonde's Smile*, 1924. Oil on canvas. 88 x 115 cm. Private collection, Paris.

69 *The Wine Bottle*, 1924. Oil on canvas. 73 x 65 cm. Fundacio Miró, Barcelona.

71 *The Carnival of Harlequin*, 1924–25. Oil on canvas. 66 x 93 cm. Allbright Knox Art Gallery, Buffalo.

73 *The Catalan*, 1925. Oil on canvas. 100 x 81 cm. Musée National d'Art Moderne, Centre Georges Pompidou, Paris.

75 *Oh! Un de ces messieurs qui a fait tout ça!* 1925. Poem painting. Oil on canvas. 130 x 95 cm. Private collection.

77   *The Siesta*, 1925. Oil on canvas. 113 x 146 cm. Musée National d'Art Moderne, Centre Georges Pompidou, Paris.

79   *This Is the Colour of My Dreams*, 1925. Poem painting. Oil on canvas. 86.5 x 129.5 cm. Collection of M. et Mme Pierre Matisse, New York.

81   *Painting,* 1926. Oil on canvas. 100 x 81 cm. Private collection. Photo: Archives Succession Miró.

83   *Painting,* 1927. Oil on canvas. 19 x 24.3 cm. Private collection. Photo: Archives Succession Miró.

85   *Landscape with Cockerel*, 1927. Oil on canvas. 130 x 195 cm. Private collection. Photo: Archives Succession Miró.

87   *Dutch Interior II*, 1928. Oil on canvas. 92 x 73 cm. Peggy Guggenheim collection, Venice. Photo: Museum of Modern Art, New York.

89   *Queen Louise of Prussia*, 1929. Oil on canvas. 81 x 100 cm. Meadows Museum, Southern University, Dallas.

91   *Portrait of Mrs Mills in 1750*, 1929. Oil on canvas. 116 x 89 cm. Museum of Modern Art, New York.

93   *Construction*, 1930. Wood and metal. 91.1 x 70.2 x 16.2 cm. Museum of Modern Art, New York. Purchase. Photograph © 1994. The Museum of Modern Art, New York.

95   *Object-Painting*, 1931. Painted wood panel with sand relief on metal-wire grill. 36 x 26 cm. Musée National d'Art Moderne, Centre Georges Pompidou, Paris.

97   *Painting*, 1933. Oil on canvas. 97 x 130 cm. Musée National d'Art Moderne, Villeneuve d'Ascq, France.

99   *Drawing-Collage (Homage to Prats)*, 1934. Collage and crayon on paper. 63.3 x 47 cm. Fundacio Miró, Barcelona.

101   *Woman*, 1934. Collage and crayon on paper velours. 106 x 70 cm. Philadelphia Museum of Art: The Louise and Walter Arensberg Collection.

103   *Aidez l'Espagne (Help Spain!)* 1937. Serigraphy. 24.8 x 19.4 cm. Private collection.

105   *Object of the Sunset*, 1938. Sculpture-object, painted tree trunk and metal elements. Musée National d'Art Moderne, Centre Georges Pompidou, Paris.

107   *A Star Caresses the Breast of a Black Woman*, 1938. Picture–poem. Oil on canvas. 129.5 x 195 cm. Tate Gallery, London.

109   *A Drop of Dew Falling from the Wing of a Bird Awakens Rosalie Sleeping in the Shadow of a Spider's Web*, 1939. Oil on canvas. 65 x 92 cm. University of Iowa Museum of Art, The Mark Ranney Memorial Fund.

111   *Constellations*, 1940–41. 45 x 38 cm. *I The Sunrise; IV Women on the Beach; XVI Woman Encircled By the Flight of a Bird; XIX Numbers and Constellations in Love with a Woman.* Private collection.

113   *Painting with Moderniste Frame*, 1943. Oil and pastels on canvas. 40 x 30 cm. Fundacio Miró, Barcelona.

115   Ceramic Plaque, 1946. Collection J. Gardy Artigas.

117   *Painting*, 1950. Oil, ropes and casa arte on canvas. 99 x 76 cm. Stedelijk Museum, Eindhoven.

119   *The Eagle Flies to the Peaks of the Mountains Hollowed Out by the Comets to Announce the Words of the Poet*, 1953. Oil on cardboard. 48 x 55 cm. Private collection. Photo: Archives Succession Miró.

121   *Self-portrait*, 1937–60. Oil and crayon on canvas. 146.5 x 96.9 cm. Fundacio Miró, Barcelona.

123   *Personage*, 1960. Painted on cardboard. 105 x 75 cm. Pierre Matisse Gallery, New York.

125   Untitled, 1967. Gouache and indian ink. 34.5 x 50 cm. Artcurial collection, Paris.

127   *The Gold of the Azure*, 1967. Oil on canvas. 205 x 173.5 cm. Fundacio Miró, Barcelona.

129   *The Wind Clock*, 1967. Bronze. 51 x 29.5 x 16 cm. Fundacio Miró, Barcelona.

131   *The Smile of the Star to the Twin Tree of the Plain*, 1968. Oil on canvas. 174 x 217 cm. Suzy and Daniel Lelong Collection, Paris. Photo: Archives Succession Miró.

133   *Lunar Bird*, 1968. Marble. 300 x 260 x 120 cm. Maeght Foundation, St Paul de Vence, France.

135   *May 1968*, 1973. Oil on canvas. 200 x 200 cm. Fundacio Miró, Barcelona.

137   *Burnt Canvas I*, 1973. Oil on ripped and burnt canvas. 130.5 x 194.6 cm. Fundacio Miró, Barcelona.

139   *Triptych for the Cell of a Condemned Man*, 1974. Oil on canvas. I: 267.3 x 351.5 cm; II: 267.3 x 351 cm; III: 267 x 350.3 cm. Fundacio Miró, Barcelona.